Praise for Princip

MW00851631

There are principles of exclusion in our society—economic, cultural, social, religious, and historical. They involve issues of race, gender, patriarchy, class, sexual orientation and disability. They are entangled in webs of social relations produced by capitalist society and they play out in government policies, both domestic and foreign. They insinuate themselves into the very grit and gristle of our everyday lives. Fortunately, we have a counterweight to these principles of exclusion in the field of education in the growing presence of principals of inclusion. These school administrators are alive and well in our schools, working tirelessly for the kind of social transformation that will enable new generations of students to participate in the benefits and resources of community, regional and national life. Darrin Griffiths' book, Principals of Inclusion, is an important testimony to the value of inclusion and provides examples of how school administrators can help to promote it. I highly recommend this book to administrators, teachers and all those who care about future generations of our youth and their well-being.

Peter McLaren, Division of Urban Schooling,
Graduate School of Education and Information Studies,
The University of California, Los Angeles.

Dr. Griffiths' *Principals of Inclusion* is both a practical, realistic blueprint and an inspiring call to action for accelerating schools/school systems in their search to optimize all students' potential (inclusion). In an information age and an increasingly interconnected Global Village, no student's potential can afford to be wasted, especially by exclusionary educational practices/traditions (either conscious or unconscious). Dr. Griffiths writes clearly, using universal metaphors/tactics applicable to all educational situations.

Doug Dunford, M.A., M.Ed., Principal, HWDSB.

This passionate insiders account will be an invaluable source of information as well as confirmation for educational practitioners.

Heidi Safia Mirza, Professor Equalities Studies in Education Institute of Education, University of London

A lucid and engaging account of robust social justice work in school administration that is grounded in lived experiences, from a dedicated school principal and intellectual whose heart, mind and actions understand equity, and who does not fall prey to the liberal myth of meritocracy. A must read for all educators and those who work in policy.

John P. Portelli, co-director, Centre for Leadership and Diversity, Ontario Institute for Studies in Education, University of Toronto

This is a most salutary contribution to current debates about how to recast education to meet the challenges of rapidly changing societies. Much recent discussion has focussed on science, technology, and preparing students to compete in globalising economies. This book takes a more holistic approach to education and educational reform. It emphasizes the role of schools, not just in providing inputs for industry and skilled workforces, but as arenas of civic engagement. It argues for culturally relevant teaching and inclusionary school practices to fulfil this role and to advance academic growth. It then draws on the experiences of its author and those of other elementary school principals to reflect on how inclusion grows in schools and to suggest leadership strategies for administrators, especially those who work in urban settings, who occupy a critical position in improving schools. Good sense and good advice!

Sandra Halperin, Department of Politics and International Relations, Royal Holloway, University of London

Principals of Inclusion is a tremendously valuable resource for school teachers and leaders as it offers us in equal measure a powerful mandate for inclusion, as well as creative, useful strategies to help us promote and assess our inclusion work. In this book Dr. Griffiths plants the seeds of inclusion, and then helps each of us each grow our own inclusion tree.

Kevin Battaglia, Principal, TDSB

Principals of Inclusion is a book that has made me stop and think. As an educator, I have promoted inclusion in the classroom, but Dr. Griffiths' book is making me ask myself whether or not I have done enough to encourage inclusion among my students. The book has also given me a better understanding of ways in which inclusion can be used successfully in hiring practices, with various cultural groups in the classroom, and indeed within the entire school environment. I consider *Principals of Inclusion* to be a valuable resource that is long overdue.

Dr. John A. Roberts, Director of Education,
Ontario Coalition of Aboriginal People

Drawing from his own experiences, as well as the perspectives of sixteen other school principals, Darrin Griffiths asks: How are we to foster a rich form of inclusion in schools? In addressing this question, he offers sound insights and practical strategies that draw from a combination of theory and practice. But this is not a catalogue of best practices. Griffiths articulates a vision of inclusion that sums up the voices of principals who feel it is important, and make it a part of their everyday lives. Inclusion, as Griffiths rightly points out, is something that is not only practiced, but is also grown and nurtured. This book would be of great value to those involved in the professional development of principals as well as to principals themselves. It would also be a useful resource for school equity committees.

Cam Cobb, Assistant Professor, University of Windsor

Dr. Griffiths has produced and articulated a powerful argument and moral message that administrators and teachers cannot ignore: the need for powerful inclusion and restating the very foundation of education, the soil in which we produce all meaningful change. The book highlights an important realization and shift in the basic foundations of why we educate. It cleverly brings to our attention that we have historically focused on unsustainable changes, ones that are often dependent on the people in place, and not the cultural environment. This book is a refreshing and invigorating response to the most pressing needs in our school system – *Principals of Inclusion* is a must read for any engaged educator, regardless of job title.

Chey Cheney, Teacher, TDSB

Principals of Inclusion is a valuable resource for school leaders who seek to advance policies relating to inclusion, social justice, equity, and diversity. Dr. Griffiths provides the context for educators to develop and implement the conditions for moving from exclusion to inclusion practices in a respectful, engaging manner. School leaders are provided with a holistic framework that explores ways to improve rates of student achievement and school-family-community engagement through culturally appropriate teaching and assessment practices.

Dr. Jenny Kay Dupuis, Member of Nipissing First Nation

As a Reading Recovery Teacher Leader reading *Principals of Inclusion* I am encouraged by the supportive administration described in this book. It is reassuring to know that many administrators realize that inclusion embraces the whole school, which includes students, parents and staff. In my current position, I am directed to promote inclusive practices in our schools. Dr. Griffiths has provided administrators and teachers alike with a tool that is easy to read and implement, which will support the goal of achieving literacy for all students. His book is a wake-up call regarding the importance of self-reflection as a means of achieving inclusionary practices for all educators.

Barb Cassar, Reading Recovery Teacher Leader, TDSB

In this text, Darrin Griffiths takes notions of social justice and inclusion from a theoretical and conceptual space to one of everyday practicality. The voices of school principals sharing their journeys to lead schools where inclusion is a central focus greatly enhances the impact this text will have on practicing and prospective school leaders. It is one of the few educational leadership texts, grounded in a critical theoretical frame, that provides the reader with practical, critically-based, day-to-day strategies to afford every child in the school a quality educational experience. This text helps to bring genuine school reform much closer to reality.

Michael E. Dantley, Ed.D., Professor and Chair
Department of Educational Leadership
School of Education, Health and Society, Miami University

Principals of Inclusion is full of the hope, possibility, power and principles of inclusive practice that educational leaders and policy makers have been looking for! A seminal work that outlines what Indigenous Elders refer to as the good path, and that we can only make by walking it and not just talking.

Dr. Jason M.C. Price
Associate Professor, Department of Curriculum and Instruction
Vice-President University of Victoria Faculty Association
Chair, UVICFA Executive Committee
Board Member, Indigenous Education Board of Advisors
Board Member, CORE Outreach Centre

Inclusion is one of the most important principles of holistic education. In this book Darrin Griffiths shows how principals can help develop inclusive schools. The book is filled with practical suggestions and includes the voices of several principals who are engaged in the processes of inclusion. Griffiths has made an important contribution as many school leaders will find this book a valuable resource in their day-to-day efforts to make their schools more holistic and inclusive.

Jack Miller,
author of The Holistic Curriculum and Whole Child Education

Principals of Inclusion:

Practical Strategies to Grow Inclusion in Urban Schools

Darrin Griffiths, Ed.D.

Foreword by
Dr. James Ryan

Afterword by
Dr. Cecilia Reynolds

Edited by Barbara Pulling
Book design by Jim Bisakowski – www.bookdesign.ca

ISBN 978-0-9918626-0-3

Word & Deed Publishing Incorporated
434-2000 Appleby Line
Burlington, Ontario, Canada, L7L 7H7

(Toll Free) 1-866-601-1213

Visit our website at
www.principalsofinclusion.com

Dedication

THIS BOOK IS DEDICATED TO my sons, Brendan and Matthew, and my wife Leslie. I wish also to acknowledge the support I received throughout this process from my mother, Marilyn Griffiths. Her ongoing encouragement and celebrations as I accomplished the various steps contributed greatly to me completing this journey. I would be remiss if I did not mention my late father, Ron Griffiths, who advocated for social justice throughout his life. As a sociology graduate from the University of Manitoba, Canada, in the 1950s, he understood that there were processes at work in society that limited the opportunities of many groups and individuals.

I want to acknowledge the impact four superb educators have had on my life. Mrs. Jeanine Avigdor and Mr. David Stone were both teachers at T.L. Kennedy Secondary School in Mississauga, Ontario, in the 1980s. Mrs. Avigdor believed that I was capable of more than what I was producing in school; she believed that I had something to offer, but needed to dedicate myself more to learning. Mr. Stone taught world issues and economic courses; I first learned from him about global inequities and injustices. He was a critical theorist who believed in social justice and inspired us to make a difference in the world. I am also indebted to Dr. Cecilia Reynolds and Dr. James Ryan for their help, guidance, and expertise through my graduate studies. Their writings, dialogues and experiences in education helped shape my thinking and vision for what schools should be doing for students.

...if a school does not stand for something more profound than raising achievement levels, then it probably does not make a memorable difference to teachers, students, or parents. Put on a spiritual plane, a school needs a deeper soul.

(Deal and Peterson 2009, Shaping School Culture: Pitfalls, Paradoxes, & Promises, 62).

Contents

Praise for Principals of Inclusion i

Dedication iii

Foreword vii

Introduction xi

Chapter 1. A Framework for Growing Inclusion 1

Chapter 2. The Process of Growing Inclusion 9

Chapter 3. The "Why": Motivators for Growing Inclusion 19

Chapter 4. Growing Inclusion with Teachers 33

Chapter 5. Growing Inclusion with Students 71

Chapter 6. Growing Inclusion with Parents 81

Chapter 7. Overcoming Barriers and Cultivating Allies 101

Chapter 8. Reconceptualising the Principalship 127

Afterword 131

References 134

Foreword

INCLUSION IS, OR AT LEAST SHOULD BE, a right for everyone. Men, women and children, regardless of their situations, lifestyles or heritages, have the right, in principle, to be included in what their communities and institutions have to offer. This means that they should be involved in decision-making and political processes, have meaningful jobs, and possess sufficient resources to allow them to participate in their communities and to be part of cultural institutions like schools. Being meaningfully included means that people have their voices heard when decisions are being made or policies instituted, have the financial resources to afford to take advantage of community opportunities, and are able to identify with what is happening in places like schools. Unfortunately, not everyone has the opportunity to be part of these practices in the same way and, as a consequence, will not share in the opportunities and rewards that accompany inclusion. Those who are not included are excluded.

Exclusion has a powerful presence. It affects deeply each and every one that it touches.

> If you have been bullied or ostracized, teased or tormented because you were too fat or skinny, too studious or too slow you ... know what it is like to be excluded. All of us have felt excluded at some time, and we all know the feelings of embarrassment and humiliation that can result. But for some people, exclusion happens every day, repeatedly and systematically. As well as hurt[ing] feelings, it destroys their opportunities and ruins their lives, especially if they are denied educational opportunities and the basic right to learn (Ryan, 2006, p. 1).

Tragically, contemporary exclusion is widespread. It infiltrates our communities and our institutions. Much of it is easy to discern. Unfortunately, however, all contemporary exclusion is not always easy to recognize or understand, particularly by those who are already included in much of what their communities and institutions have to offer. Alexander (2012), for example, claims that current colour-blind sensibilities have obscured the fact that people of colour continue to be excluded from current social institutions. Indeed, the judicial system routinely treats people of African heritage differently than it does white people, both in the United States and in Canada. And so this complicates matters for those who promote inclusion. Not only will they have their work cut out for them as they try to convince others of the value of inclusion, they will also have to be even more vigilant in identifying the increasing number of subtle forms of exclusion.

Nowhere is exclusion more challenging to discern than in education. While overt exclusive practices were routine at one time, most contemporary rhetoric descries exclusive educational practices (like segregation policies, for example) and supports inclusion. The irony, however, is that many inclusive-sounding policies may actually be exclusive. For example, crucial elements of the American *No Child Left Behind* (NCLB) policy are decidedly exclusive. Standardized testing, a commonplace practice in most public school systems in Canada and the Western world and an integral part of NCLB, is exclusive. The tests generally display a uniquely Western cultural perspective, leaving those not familiar with it excluded from the sense of the associated test questions (Ryan, 2012). Exclusion also occurs in the preparation for these tests; schools may focus their test preparation only on those students they believe have the best chance to do well on the test, leaving others excluded (Darling-Hammond, 2010; Hursh, 2007). Finally, schools may manoeuvre to exclude certain less able students from the test, thereby increasing school scores. This may involve expanding the numbers of students classified as "special," or simply keeping other students from proceeding into the testing grade (Hursh, 2007). Hardest hit by these exclusive tests are low-income and non-white students (Darling-Hammond, 2010).

Despite the exclusive nature of this testing, it continues to proliferate, its exclusive character hidden from view, drowned out by the voices of proponents of the tests, who claim that standardized testing enables schools and systems to hold educators, schools and school systems accountable for what they do, that it ensures that students are exposed to essential knowledge, and guarantees that they improve their learning. So successfully has the case for standardized testing been made that today it is almost taken for granted that test scores on standardized tests are synonymous with student learning. Unfortunately, the exclusive character of the tests gets lost in all of this noise. Even proponents of inclusion may find it difficult to see exclusion in the tests, much less argue against their exclusive nature.

Given the intractability and imperceptible nature of contemporary exclusion in communities and schools, it is vital that educators champion inclusion. No one is more important in this endeavour than the principal. Principals can be the most influential individuals in their schools. However, it is not an easy thing for principals, or other educators, to recognize, understand and do something about exclusion. They are busy people and, as I have illustrated above, exclusion is not always easy to understand, much less prevent. This is why Darrin Griffiths' book, *Principals of Inclusion,* is so timely. It provides principals with a framework for doing something about this often-invisible menace.

Principals of Inclusion speaks directly to principals. It is written in easily accessible prose and focuses on topics that concern contemporary principals. Its author is well equipped to do so. A practicing principal with plenty of experience, Dr. Griffiths knows what is important in administrators' work. He recounts many of his experiences in ways that are instructive. But readers can learn from more than just his wisdom. He also tells the stories of many of his principal brethren who describe how they came to value inclusion, what difficulties they experience in their inclusive work, and how they accomplish their inclusive goals.

Employing the metaphor of a growing tree, Dr. Griffiths helps readers understand the nature of inclusion and, just as importantly, how they can promote it. From nurturing the soil to developing the branches of the tree, principals have an important role to play in the practices of inclusion in their respective schools. The book helps educators understand inclusion and provides advice on how principals can help others understand inclusion and, by extension, how they can recognize these often-invisible forms of exclusion in everyday practices. The accounts of how the principals came to value inclusion will help readers understand some of the less visible guises that exclusion can take and why inclusion is a preferable alternative.

The bulk of the book is taken up with practical suggestions about what principals can do to promote inclusion in their schools. An important part of these strategies includes helping others to understand exclusion and inclusion. The author provides readers with examples of how to share views with staff, how to discuss inclusion, generate resources, invite guest speakers to raise awareness of exclusion, and how to help staff, students and parents understand it. The book also provides principals with many ideas for putting inclusion into practice. These include modeling behaviour, assisting with the development of suitable pedagogies and assessments, encouraging leadership among students, teachers and parents, providing dialogue opportunities, sharing decision-making with others, and devising strategies to deal with the many obstacles that get in the way of these practices. Dr. Griffiths and the principals who speak provide a wealth of potential strategies for principals to use.

Darrin Griffith's book, *Principals of Inclusion*, is a must read for administrators who are interested in promoting inclusion in their schools and communities. It will surely help those educators who are serious about inclusion to understand it and do something about promoting and extending it.

James Ryan
Ontario Institute for Studies in Education

References

Alexander, Michelle. 2012. *The new Jim Crow: Mass incarceration in the age of colorblindness*. New York: The New Press.

Darling-Hammond, Linda. 2010. *The flat world and education: How America's commitment to equity will determine our future*. New York: Teachers College Press.

Hursh, David. 2007. "Assessing No Child Left Behind and the rise of neoliberal educational policies". *American Educational Research Journal* 44 (3), 493-518.

Ryan, James. 2006. *Inclusive leadership*. San Francisco, CA: Jossey-Bass.

------ 2012. *Struggling for inclusion: Leadership in a neoliberal world*. Charlotte, NC: Information Age.

Introduction

SITTING IN MY OFFICE ONE AFTERNOON after a particularly long day, I reflected on whether the students in my elementary school would be ready to confront the world outside, with all its defects and barriers, after graduation. Would those who didn't fit into the traditional definition of privilege in North America be able to manoeuvre through the educational system and meet their full potential as learners and as human beings?

When I began my career as an elementary school teacher in 1993, as a white, heterosexual, middle-class male of Anglo-European heritage, I believed that North America was a meritocracy. All students had an equal chance of success, I thought, if they followed the rules of the system and worked hard. People who didn't experience success in school – or in life, for that matter – simply hadn't followed the rules or worked hard enough.

But my years of working in schools have dramatically altered this belief. I now understand that many students are excluded from such chances of success for reasons that have nothing to do with "merit." Moreover, the educational system is not structured or organized to ensure equitable opportunities for all students. As a teacher, I learned very quickly that students and their parents were excluded from school for a myriad of reasons. It was in my transition from teacher to administrator, however, that I began to see both exclusionary school-wide practices and the possibilities for changing them. Many students and families expressed feelings of isolation and marginalization. They did not see themselves reflected in the way we "did business." I came to believe that these students and their parents were right. While as staff we had modified the techniques of instruction, we had not addressed the core societal issues, such as racism, sexism, and classism, that support continuing patterns of exclusion and oppression in our schools.

One of the central tensions all administrators contend with is this: how do we support the diverse needs of our students in the context of an educational system that can be characterized as hyper-accountable, with its exhaustive reliance and emphasis on test scores? There is also significant pressure on administrators to ensure that these test scores improve each year. This kind of pressure has limited our peripheral vision; we have been conditioned by a laser-like focus on quantitative data. Make no mistake: it is hugely important that our students become literate readers and writers. But there are equally important components that merit discussion and application. Experienced administrators will remember the days when we took a more holistic approach to the purpose of education, and that's the approach I'll be advocating for in the pages that follow. As Miller (1993) outlines, holistic education

> …nurtures the development of the whole person; it is concerned with the intellectual as well as emotional, social, physical, creative/intuitive, aesthetic, and spiritual potentials (79).

A holistic focus endeavours to encompass the many different domains – talents, beliefs, experiences, histories – of what makes us human. Conventional education reproduces the dominant culture, while the holistic approach challenges the status quo.

As educators, how can we ensure that all participants are genuinely involved and engaged in school governance and practice? In this book, I'll make the argument that inclusive leadership can show us the way; with its roots in social justice, it is directly applicable to serving our diverse students' needs. Inclusive leadership has at its core the conviction that all participants' voices and experiences are essential. There is no overarching template, since no two schools' needs are the same. But inclusive leadership, within the larger framework of what I call "growing inclusion," can serve as a guide and be an indispensable tool in supporting the long-term sustainability of our schools.

My interest in both inclusion and the leadership to achieve it is rooted in my twenty years of experience in education – the past thirteen in administration – working in five elementary schools in some of the poorest areas of two large North American cities. Schools are complex entities, but I am optimistic that change can and will occur. In fact, there is simply too much at stake for change *not* to happen. It is this sense of urgency that fuels my goal of achieving inclusion in urban elementary schools.

My quest to support my students, parents and staff started with enrolling part-time in a doctoral program. I wanted to learn how my world-view and biases were affecting my attitude and my actions, because it was critical that change begin with me. The program also afforded me opportunities to learn from many talented and innovative principals who are powerful advocates for social justice. While I knew from experience that certain students' chances at school were limited by factors beyond their control, I wanted to understand more comprehensively what lay at the root of their exclusion.

This book draws on both my doctoral research and my own experiences as an elementary principal. I've written it for school administrators, especially those who work in urban settings. Despite the overwhelming demands of the job, we occupy a critical position in improving schools and, most importantly, in supporting all of our students.

As part of my research, I interviewed sixteen other urban elementary principals to discover how they promoted inclusion in their schools. The principals you'll hear from in this book are highly regarded by their colleagues for their dedication to social justice, particularly inclusion. Too often the voices of principals are absent within the vast domain of leadership research; I hope that this book will address to some extent those omissions. I hope, too, that their experiences will speak to you and win you over to the ranks of those striving to make inclusion a reality in our schools.

In the North American context, inclusion is most often associated with special education students (Ware 1995, 127). But there is a growing body of research that applies the goal of inclusion to all students. For the purposes of this book, I define inclusion as "a philosophy that brings diverse students, families, educators, and community members together to create schools and other social institutions based on acceptance, belonging and community" (Bloom, Permutter, and Burnell in Salend 2005, 6). Inclusion is now associated with full-scale reform that "incorporates all children and youths as active, fully participating members of the school community; that views diversity as the norm" (Ferguson 1996, 17).

In his examination of how listening and inclusion are related, Veck (2009) asks a crucial question: How might both educators and students be included in an organization so that they are "of" and not merely "in" it? (141). This idea has become central to how I see my role and responsibilities as a principal. Students and staff members who are simply "in" a school do little more than occupy space: they have no voice or input into school practices or structures. I am interested in the "of" aspect of inclusion, extending this notion into a practice whereby all school participants have input and ongoing opportunities to create, shape, and determine how the school operates.

As I have reflected on how inclusion grows in schools, it has occurred to me that the complex process aligns with the living structure of a tree, specifically in the interdependence of the soil, the seed, the roots, the trunk, the branches, and the leaves. For a tree to thrive, all of these elements must work in concert; no single element can sustain growth. This also holds true for growing inclusion: many different steps, participants, and practices are necessary to sustain and develop it. No principal working alone can ensure that inclusion takes hold; the process demands that many individuals and many roles work together. The analogy of the tree also underlines the importance of sustainability. Many elementary administrators do not stay much longer than five years in one school. Depending on system or district needs, an administrator will sometimes be moved to a new school much earlier than that.

The first few times I introduced the concept of inclusion into a school, I wondered if the practices we had instituted would continue once I was transferred. In most cases they didn't, because I had focussed too much on the "branches" of the tree – the practices and strategies for growing inclusion. I now understand the importance of devoting more time from the onset to exploring the "soil" – the purpose of education – and developing an understanding of the "trunk" – the reason or the rationale for growing inclusion – with all staff members. Staff members may follow the practices of inclusion, but unless practices are plumbed at the moral level, staff will not develop the critical consciousness necessary to sustain them. Concentrating on the soil and the trunk supports the long-term growth of inclusion.

Growing inclusion in an elementary school is a complicated, uneven process that requires daily dedication. While I don't subscribe to the singular or "hero-leader" notion of leadership, I do know that for inclusive practices to become part of a school's culture, the principal must take the lead. Everyone must be involved for inclusion to work, and there are no quick fixes, shortcuts or simple recipes that will achieve long-term sustainability. But growing inclusion cannot happen without the principal being its fiercest and most persistent advocate, especially in the beginning stages.

Inclusion and exclusion in our society are directly connected with notions of power and privilege. Simply put, the dominant group in society determines which experiences, knowledge, and histories are valued. The dominant culture in North America, despite rapidly changing demographics, continues to comprise individuals with white skin, of European descent, who speak English, and are male, able-bodied and middle-class. There is a mountain of literature outlining how these constructs allow certain individuals to limit and oppress others. Inclusion in schools benefits staff members, students, and parents, and it can counter the societal forces that marginalize non-dominant-culture individuals.

Staff members

Staff members, particularly teachers, are the key players in determining how students fare in schools. Involving teachers in making change directly supports the development, growth, and sustainability of professional learning communities. Inclusion demands that all staff members' voices, histories, experiences and expertise influence how the school operates and, most importantly, how interactions with students take place.

In this book, I use Hord's (1997) definition of a successful learning community: "one in which the teachers in a school and its administrators continually seek and share learning, and act on their learning" (in Zepeda, 2004). This does not mean the principal or an individual teacher instructing others; it means all staff members sharing ideas on how to support students in the school in a holistic way. An effective professional learning community must do more than simply follow prevailing pedagogical practices and high-yield strategies. On the continuum of teaching and learning, a holistic approach involves sharing expertise and craft knowledge that support students in navigating an oppressive, marginalizing society, and developing a critical understanding of the world. Matthews and Crow (2010) posit that current accountability trends in education place emphasis on specific scores or levels of achievement in literacy and numeracy while ignoring the "social, emotional, and civic engagement" of students (119-120). Inclusion moves beyond commonly held notions of teaching and learning to encompass all of these things.

Students

Students who are not part of the dominant culture are excluded from realizing their full potential and humanity in all societal institutions, including schools. Students who are non-white, female, gay, lesbian or transgendered, poor, differently abled, or from families who speak English as a second language, have to overcome many barriers to find success in the educational system (Ryan 2003, 2006abc). And those students who are not successful in the educational system are at a great disadvantage in terms of making their way in the world. Both quantitative and qualitative research have shown that exclusionary practices are powerful determinants of not only how students fare in schools but of how they see themselves as people.

Parents

There is a wealth of research documenting the impact parental involvement has on student achievement (Olender et al., 2010; Ferlazzo and Hammond 2009; Grant and Ray, 2010). Getting parents and guardians involved in the school is no easy task, especially when those individuals have experienced marginalization and exclusion as students themselves. Including parents and guardians in schools, then, is vital for two reasons: it promotes student achievement and it helps the school to identify and correct exclusionary practices and structures.

Principals

All school administrators face an increasing load of tasks, pressures, and expectations. The current reality in education is that emphasis is placed strictly on students' academic achievement and their scores on standardized tests. Unfortunately, this imperative dominates the agendas of many administrators (Quinn 2002, 19). In this model, the priority for principals is instructional leadership; the principal must ensure that his or her students make academic progress, and this creates high levels of personal stress. As Cushing et al. (2003) argue,

> [s]tress comes from high levels of responsibility while authority and flexibility are simultaneously reduced via union contracts and fiscal and legal requirements. It comes from being the first head to roll if reform demands and targets aren't met (29).

Despite these increased stresses and demands, however, we must endeavour as principals to support all of our students' diverse needs through inclusive leadership. My argument here is simple: only inclusion supports true academic growth.

Traditional leadership approaches place much importance on the hero-leader who uses positional power or character traits to influence staff members and the school community. Democratic leadership theories move away from the hero-leader toward collective decision-making and a sharing of power within the school. Inclusive leadership, as posited by James Ryan, is part of the social justice paradigm. It supports the purpose of education with a focus on: 1) each student being seen as an end in him/herself; 2) commitment to each student's social, moral, emotional, and academic development; 3) the stated goal of supporting each student in developing a critical eye regarding how the world operates; and 4) an ongoing process that ensures students from diverse backgrounds and cultures are meaningfully included in school activities.

The need for inclusion is greatest in our urban schools. Urban schools in North America contend with issues of poverty and race, and serve families who have been marginalized economically and socially (Russo and

Cooper 1999; Fossey 2003; Daniel 2007). Many large urban centres in the United States have suffered economically due to "white flight," which involves white middle-class families moving to the suburbs (Anyon 1997; Fossey 2003; Anyon 2005; Theobald 2005; Loder 2006). Urban areas in Canada share many of the same challenges. The majority of people new to the country settle in cities, and there has been a significant increase in the cultural and ethnic diversity of Canada's population (McGahan 1995). The percentage of people living in poverty in Canadian urban areas has increased (Kazemipur and Halli 2000; Le, 2000). As educators, we need to address these related factors that can limit students' opportunities for success.

While most of this book will be devoted to the "how" of inclusion – practices and strategies – the vital building blocks depend on the "why." For me, the "why" took the form of a personal awakening. Once I began to understand how our current system constrains opportunities for so many, while allowing others a much greater chance of success, I could not look at the world in the same way. I now understand that, far from being immune to societal methods of exclusion, schools have long been a force in replicating the very injustices that education aims to eliminate.

My "why" propels me to work toward making schools inclusive places for all children. I've learned, too, that there is a direct relationship between the strength engendered by knowledge of the "why" and the energy to fight back. Learning about the system strengthens our "why," which in turn gives us the impetus to challenge the inequities within our schools. The "why" can give us purpose and fuel for action. It is our anchor for decision-making and our internal check when it comes to the choices we make every day as administrators. Fullan (2011) writes,

> ...when passion comes alive – when it turns out to be a powerful driver – it is in situations where we actually accomplish something of high moral value, which in turn energizes us to do even more (23).

Understanding and acting on this "why" is of high moral value for us as administrators. All children deserve the opportunity to be genuinely included in their school, and long after we leave our current schools, it is the "why" that will stay with those we have worked alongside.

Our students depend on us to make decisions that will provide them with opportunities for success now and in the future. Only the genuine inclusion of all school participants can make this a reality. We need a practical structure to begin this important work, and in this book I offer such a plan for doing that.

CHAPTER 1

A Framework for Growing Inclusion

> Though I do not believe that a plant will spring up where
> no seed has been, I have great faith in a seed. Convince me
> that you have a seed there, and I am prepared to expect
> wonders. (Henry David Thoreau)

GROWING INCLUSION IN SCHOOLS involves six main interrelated
components. Each of them is critical for long-term success. I like to use the
analogy of a tree. Inclusion, like a tree, depends for its strength and health
on the soil, the seed, the roots, the trunk, the branches and the leaves.

1) The Soil: The Purpose of Education

Without the proper soil, a tree will not grow. Without a clear understanding of the purpose of education, inclusion will not grow either. A solid
grounding in the soil will anchor our thoughts and beliefs about what education can do and should be doing for our students.

The purpose of education is much more than simply training students to
read, write and perform well on standardized tests. An inclusive definition
contains four key elements.

i) Students are ends in themselves. Students are not just future workers in
training; they are individuals with particular histories, talents, hopes, and
beliefs. Yet the incredible pressure on schools today to improve test results
nearly always comes at the cost of seeing the students in a limiting way.
Inclusion depends on schools adapting and changing to support the needs

of students, not on students conforming to the traditional practices and knowledge systems of the school.

ii) The goals of education are holistic. A holistic approach recognizes education as a synthesis, in which personal, social, and moral development are key. It is crucial that schools promote, more than simply assess, the intellectual growth of students. Without multifaceted support, many students will fail to reach their potential as contributing citizens in a pluralistic democracy.

iii) Education should prepare students to understand and shape the world. Smith et al. (1998) assert that the primary purpose of education is to prepare students to understand and shape the world (in Portelli and Solomon 2001). In order to do that, students need to learn how the identities of individuals and groups are socially constructed and maintained through various forms of communication and practice. Are students able to discern how race, gender, sexual orientation, etcetera, are applied through practices in our institutions, including in schools? Do they understand how to challenge the systems that maintain privilege for certain groups and individuals?

Helping students to develop a critical eye aligns neatly with the inclusive purpose of education. Non-dominant-culture students, when they encounter exclusionary barriers, need to understand why and how those forces operate. This knowledge will help them to navigate societal complexities while, at the same time, limiting their internalizing of societal stereotypes and messages.

iv) All students are included. Too often democracy in schools is defined as the "majority rules." That's not the kind of democracy I'm aiming for as an educator. Instead, when we're making decisions or having a discussion, I want continually to ask whose voice is missing. For example, the current composition of a student council or leadership group might not reflect the diversity of the school. In an inclusive culture, all voices are represented.

2) The Seed: An Inclusive Vision for Your School

Rooted in the soil, the seed in this analogy is an inclusive vision for your school that is specific to the needs of students, staff members, and parents. A vision like this is both utopian and pragmatic: in a perfect world, what would make all of the groups involved feel they are "of" the school and not merely "in" it?

Here's an example drawn from my current experience of working in a school with a significant number of Aboriginal students. Our long-term goal is that Aboriginal students will see themselves reflected in all aspects of the school, be it physical structure, curriculum, events, pedagogy or daily practices. Our goal for the first year was to ensure that all classrooms had at least one daily practice that acknowledged or was based on Aboriginal teachings. Staff, students, and parents provided input, and we backward-mapped from our long-term goal to see what the short-term steps would be. The seed was our collective vision for our students. Our goals were specific to those students, and they aligned with the soil, the inclusive purpose of education.

3) The Roots: The Sources of Information to Support Your Knowledge and Understanding of Inclusion.

Roots derive nourishment from the soil and deliver that nourishment to the tree. They are the highways that continually support information moving back and forth between the soil and the trunk. Using my analogy, the roots supply evidence to support the "why," the rationale for promoting inclusion in schools. These roots can include personal stories of inclusion and/or exclusion; ongoing dialogue with students, parents, and staff members about issues of equity and social justice, specifically those relating to inclusion; readings in critical social and educational theory; the gathering of both qualitative and quantitative information about student achievement; and personal reflections on how the school is meeting the needs of students, parents and staff. This list is not exhaustive, but all of these elements will serve to feed and nourish the tree.

Continuing with the example of my current school, the roots are: 1) knowledge of Aboriginal histories, cultures, languages, and experiences; 2) awareness of Aboriginal people's oppression, both past and present; 3) readings in critical theory on the subject; 4) ongoing dialogue with Aboriginal staff members, students, parents, and community members; and 5) data generated from report card marks, reading levels, attendance, and secondary school graduation rates. All of these roots supply the trunk – our "why" for inclusion – with crucial information.

4) The Trunk: The "Why" of Inclusion

The trunk nourishes the whole tree, allowing the branches to grow and expand. In my analogy, the trunk represents the "why" of inclusion: our reason for promoting inclusion, with specific reference to students and their families. The "why" comes from us, as educators, understanding the social and political complexities involved. The "why" for promoting inclusion for Aboriginal students in my current school is that after hundreds of years of forced assimilation of their people by Western dominant culture, many students are not aware of their cultures, their histories, or their people's traditional teachings. In other words, many of the Aboriginal students do not know who they are.

Fed by the roots – our knowledge and understanding – the trunk is strengthened by our passion for growing inclusion.

5) The Branches: Strategies and Practices for Growing Inclusion

In this analogy, the branches represent the "how" of inclusion. Each branch represents a strategy or practice used to achieve our goal. The strength and reach of these branches depend on our clear understanding of why inclusion is important.

6) The Leaves: The Individuals included in your school.

The leaves represent the individuals included and are directly connected to the branches – practices or strategies. Visualizing, engaging with, and analyzing these can determine whether our strategies are actually working.

The six components described above – the soil, the seed, the roots, the trunk, the branches and the leaves – will give you a framework for growing inclusion in your school. In the next chapter, I'll describe the process for getting that framework in place.

———•·•———

A Framework for Growing Inclusion in Schools

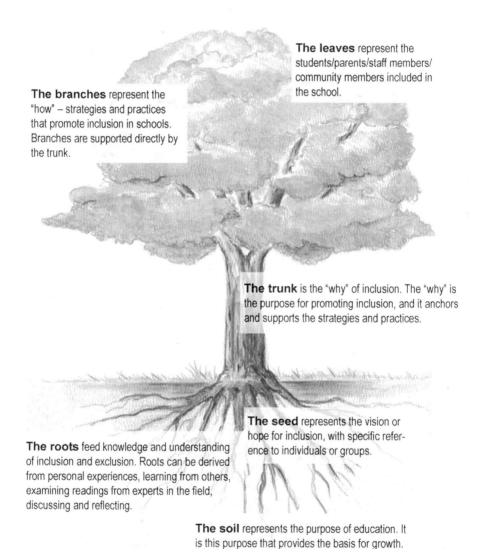

The leaves represent the students/parents/staff members/ community members included in the school.

The branches represent the "how" – strategies and practices that promote inclusion in schools. Branches are supported directly by the trunk.

The trunk is the "why" of inclusion. The "why" is the purpose for promoting inclusion, and it anchors and supports the strategies and practices.

The roots feed knowledge and understanding of inclusion and exclusion. Roots can be derived from personal experiences, learning from others, examining readings from experts in the field, discussing and reflecting.

The seed represents the vision or hope for inclusion, with specific reference to individuals or groups.

The soil represents the purpose of education. It is this purpose that provides the basis for growth.

A Framework for Growing Inclusion in Schools:
School-based example

The branches i) provide ongoing forums for Aboriginal students, parents, staff and community members to share their thoughts about the school; **ii)** use staff experts to share knowledge of Aboriginal cultures and students with all staff members; **iii)** have community based programs that directly support Aboriginal people in the school; **iv)** Utilize Aboriginal experts to develop student leadership groups; **v)** Connect curriculum with Aboriginal histories, cultures, experiences, etc.

The leaves represent the Aboriginal students/parents/staff members/community members

The trunk: Aboriginal cultures and histories have been oppressed and marginalized by dominant white European cultures. Aboriginal school participants' experiences, histories, and cultures are not represented in the school.

The roots: ongoing dialogues with Aboriginal students, staff members, parents, community members; guidance from scholars and experts in the field who understand both the historical and current context; reading in critical theory; examination of the quantitative data (report cards, reading levels, attendance, etc.).

The seed: Aboriginal histories, cultures, languages, experiences must be incorporated into the school.

The soil: students as ends in themselves; students able to understand and to shape their world; goals of education are holistic; all students are included.

The Process of Growing Inclusion

School leaders need to embody a social justice consciousness within their belief systems or values. This includes needing to possess a deep understanding of power relations and social construction including white privilege, heterosexism, poverty, misogyny, and ethnocentrism. (Capper et al. 2006, 213)

THE PROCESS OF GROWING INCLUSION ACTIVELY involves parents, staff, and students, since long-term sustainability depends on all individuals being genuinely included in the school. While there is a process to growing inclusion, it is not a linear one. You'll experience many starts, stops, and changes of direction as ideas and practices are refined. The process of growing inclusion is contextual, and it varies according to the backgrounds and experiences of your students, your staff members, and other members of the school community.

The Process Starts with Us

The process of inclusion begins with the principal. To be effective in this kind of leadership, we need to reflect first on our own experiences, biases, and possible privilege so that we truly understand the concepts of inclusion and exclusion.

Never having experienced systemic exclusion myself, I was not aware initially of how schools could oppress and marginalize students who were different from me. Like many other people from privileged groups, I was largely unaware of my own privilege (Goodman 2001, 24). Diangelo (2006), for example, posits that whites "are taught to see their perspectives as objective and representative of reality" (216). School administrators are no different; we make sense of our reality based on our own history and background, our circle of friends and associates, and our work history (Evans 2007, 162). This is problematic, though, given that most elementary principals in North America still belong to the dominant culture.

When I came to examine my own privilege, I realized first of all that my skin colour has afforded me many benefits. McIntosh (1989) writes,

> I have come to see white privilege as an invisible package of unearned assets that I can count on cashing in each day, but about which I was "meant" to remain oblivious. White privilege is like an invisible weightless knapsack of special provisions, maps, passports, codebooks, visas, clothes, tools, and blank checks (10).

Ken, a teacher of African heritage, told me in conversation one day that he viewed "whiteness" as a passport through society; being white allowed people to travel and interact freely. His skin colour, on the other hand, drew glances, stares, and other non-verbal signs of not being welcome or accepted. Ken's experiences were magnified when he and his wife were travelling together or simply out on the town for a walk; his wife held a passport of whiteness, and he did not. Ken's story is a powerful reminder that people's experiences in society differ, based on their skin colour, height, weight, gender, language, age, and other characteristics. Ken's analogy of the passport made the experience of discrimination visible and real to me.

My roots of learning about exclusion have been three-fold: 1) conversations with students and their families; 2) readings in critical theory as applied to schools; and 3) knowledge shared by outstanding school principals.

My experiences as a teacher and principal in five "inner-city" schools over nearly twenty years gave me the first inkling that North America was not the meritocracy I had thought. It was clear that students experienced school differently, depending on the colour of their skin, how much money their parent or parents earned, whether they spoke the language of instruction, whether they were male or female, how we as educators conceptualized their potential, and whether their learning styles "fit" the program of instruction in the class. The established hierarchies of class, race, and deficit thinking, with their accompanying low expectations of those on the wrong side of the line, combined to convince me that hard work on its own would not ensure success.

I sought out critical theory to help me understand what I was experiencing in the schools. Critical theorists examine the assumptions and beliefs that provide the basis for the oppression of people and suggest solutions (Martusewicz and Reynolds 1994; Robinson 1994; Alway 1995; Popkewitz 1999; Wotherspoon 2004). I began reading authors such as Michael Apple, Henry Giroux, Michael Dantley, Jean Anyon, James Ryan, Peter McLaren, bell hooks, John Portelli, Joseph Murphy, and Paolo Freire, all of whom infuse critical theory into education. Critical theory supported my lived reality as an educator working in urban schools, and helped to illuminate the deeper issues of oppression and marginalization that are part and parcel of the system. I understood that these deeper issues could not be remedied strictly by improving pedagogical practices; systemic changes were required. It was uncomfortable to consider that perhaps my success in completing school could be attributed to factors other than just my hard work; that it could be attributed to my white skin, gender, and middle-class background. I also came to realize how damaging the notion of meritocracy is, since it places blame squarely on the shoulders of the individual, without examination of the larger system. As Cooper, He and Levin (2011) assert,

> meritocracy can lead to students losing their motivation or giving up and dropping out when they feel they cannot succeed because of their color, their lack of English skills, of their status as residents of particular neighborhoods; and many educators think they just aren't trying hard enough (15).

When students and their families believe their lack of success is due to something inherent in who they are as people, instead of to an oppressive, unfair, and marginalizing system, these "deficit ideologies" become self-fulfilling prophecies, perpetuating the hoax that certain groups are inferior to the dominant norm or group.

Once I began my doctoral research, I learned a lot from my contact with exceptional principals who were seeking social justice through inclusion. Each of them had developed approaches specific to their own schools and student populations.

As a principal today, I continue to engage these three roots of learning, both because understanding is ongoing, and because I need to revisit my privilege often so I do not become lost again. Schools should be powerful forces in challenging the status quo and ensuring that all individuals have opportunities to engage in education. Change depends on us, as principals, to first question how we view the world. Once we're committed to that, we are ready to begin the process of growing inclusion.

Growing Inclusion in Your School

The diagram on the next page uses the tree analogy to illustrate the process of growing inclusion. The soil is the centre of the process, because our collective beliefs and understanding fuel the growth of inclusion. Ensuring that the soil is ready can be the most challenging part of this process.

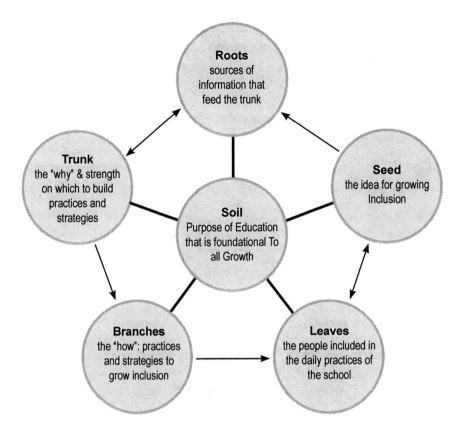

1) **Prepare the Soil:** As noted, using the tree analogy, the soil represents the purpose of education. This is a subject that you and your staff members will want to reflect on and discuss. Creating a mission statement for your school is critically important in order to keep your goals and actions aligned and get all participants in sync. As DuFour and Eaker (1998) assert,

> The sine qua non of a learning community is shared understandings and common values. What separates a learning community from an ordinary school is its collective commitment to guiding principles that articulate what the people in the school believe and what they seek to create (25).

Your mission statement identifies the core beliefs and commitments of your school. As Vojtek and Vojtek (2009) argue, establishing clarity of purpose and direction through a mission statement will also guide staff members' choices (75).

As noted, prior to tabling these questions for discussion with your staff, it is important for you to reflect on them yourself.

To get the process started, here are some guiding questions for you to use in self-reflection and to discuss with your staff:

1. *What is our purpose here at _____ school?*

2. *What kind of difference do we want to make? What role do we want to play in students' lives?*

3. *What are the most important things we can do for our students?*

4. *What constitutes a "good" education?*

These questions are broad, but they will help you get to the core of the purpose of education for your school. Keep in mind that staff members will need ample time to discuss these things in small groups, and then as a collective, returning to these questions over a number of weeks. The discussions should yield responses that identify the well-being of students on all levels: moral, physical, and social. The resulting mission statement will give you a starting point, and it can be revisited whenever information, knowledge, or expertise levels change.

2) Plant the Seed. Using the tree analogy, the seed is the vision of inclusion you develop for your school, based specifically on the needs of your students. Each school is different, and the seed comes from knowing your students and their families. Here are a few guiding questions to help you and your staff clarify your mission for the school.

i) *What do we know about our students' lives, in terms of their experiences, cultures, histories, etcetera?*

ii) *Whose voices are present and whose are missing from discussions about how our school operates?*

iii) *What do our students and their families think about the school in all aspects? Do they feel welcome, included, and "of" the school?* (The answers to these questions can be gleaned through informal discussion, surveys, anecdotal observations, quantitative data on achievement, historical information regarding participation in the school, and the examination of school clubs, programs, and pedagogical supports.)

iv) *What do the critical theorists and researchers suggest about the systemic biases and barriers pertaining to your students and families?*

This gathering of information and the subsequent discussions will take time, but the more you know about your students, the faster this part of the process will go. What is the information you gathered indicating that you need to do as a school? As a school community? The answers to these two questions will help you construct your specific focus, or seed, for growing inclusion. A seed statement should be brief, direct, and simple to understand for all school participants.

3) Identify the Roots. What are the sources that will provide you with the information you need to support your specific goal for inclusion (the seed). At my current school, we identified the initial roots as Aboriginal students, parents, community members, university researchers and experts. Since our focus is on including our Aboriginal learners and their families, we needed to ask them directly how they viewed the school, with specific reference to whether they felt included or valued. Those who serve as roots not only provide initial information but can also provide updates and often become powerful allies in nurturing the growth of inclusion. At my current school, five to seven parents, numerous students, and a few community members provide ongoing input and feedback to school staff members on how things are going.

4) Construct the Trunk – the "Why." The "why," as outlined in your purpose and rationale for growing inclusion, is the passion that fuels your efforts. The information gathered from your roots will show you why inclusion is necessary. At my school, the students and adults who acted as roots shared numerous experiences of marginalization and oppression at the elementary school level. They felt that their histories, knowledge bases, and experiences were not valued or infused into the curriculum, and that their voices were not heard or considered important. Our qualitative research was supplemented by numerous academic journal articles and books that examined how Aboriginal students and their families have been oppressed. At this step of the process, you are "making the case" for inclusion in your school, with specific reference to your students' needs. Understanding the "why" will motivate everyone toward the end goal of inclusion.

5) The Branches. The branches represent the strategies and methods you employ to grow inclusion. As outlined, the branches are the "how" of inclusion, and they are where the hard practical work of inclusion begins. Each branch represents one strategy or practice and should align with the focus of your seed – your specific goal related to inclusion.

For example, at my current school we wanted to increase the number of parents attending our early-years evening meetings. In the past these meetings had been poorly attended, and those who did attend were not representative of the diverse student population. We used a number of strategies to increase attendance: 1) sending letters home with students; 2) calling parents to personally welcome them; 3) posting messages on the school billboard; 4) having additional staff meet and greet parents before and after school on the playground; 5) providing snacks for all participants; 6) offering prizes and take-home resources that aligned with the evening meeting. Our meeting numbers doubled as a result of these strategies. And even as we made gains, we continued to ask ourselves two important questions: "Whose voice was missing from the meeting tonight?" and "Did the participants represent the diversity in the school?"

Make no mistake: this is an ongoing process, some strategies will work right away; others may never work, despite many attempts. At my school, we often found that something we considered an excellent strategy resulted in little or no change to the number of individuals included. It all comes down to knowing who your students, parents and staff members are; you will need to identify and implement many different strategies to achieve your goal.

6) The Leaves. The leaves on each branch represent the individuals who are included as a result of the strategy represented by that branch. In the example I mentioned above, the attendance at our early-years meetings doubled as a result of our efforts. Another example: we wanted to attract parents to our parent council meetings, especially those who had not been represented in previous years. The strategies we devised yielded three more members who began to attend on a regular basis.

The process of growing inclusion begins with us as principals. It can be tempting to move directly to the strategies and practices, but it's important to engage everyone in your school in the process I've outlined. That way, the long-term growth won't be compromised the moment you move to your next school. Self-reflection and shared understanding of the "why" – the rationale for growing inclusion – will fuel inclusive actions in your school. In the next chapter, we'll hear from a number of principals on the sources of their own passion for inclusion.

The "Why": Motivators for Growing Inclusion

THE PRINCIPALS I CONSULTED during my doctoral research were all motivated to grow and promote inclusion their schools. Most of them had developed their passion, purpose, and rationale for growing inclusion early in their lives. Their own experiences shaped their perceptions and understanding of how inclusion and exclusion work in our society.

Personal or Familial Exclusion Growing Up

Childhood experiences gave some of the principals I spoke to personal insight into how it feels to be excluded and the profound impact it has. Nigel, for instance, was very aware, growing up in a working-class home, that his family was not to provide the same opportunities as families who were more secure financially. His father discussed these societal inequalities with his children so that Nigel gained a strong understanding of the lived repercussions of class structure. As he told me,

> I certainly was aware of the fact that life wasn't fair and that the class structure was a pretty dominant piece in our lives. But you know, the fact that hardly anybody went to university from my school, that was a pretty clear picture.

Nigel's father died when Nigel was still young, and the family went on welfare. "The system was just not designed for people like me [on welfare] to do well," he told me. But this early instruction on class structure empowered Nigel and provided him with a lens through which to understand the world. This education was, in many ways, his father's legacy. Nigel has applied his father's teachings throughout his life and uses them today, as a principal, to advocate for students.

Dave grew up in New York City and lived there until his parents divorced. When his mother remarried a number of years later and they moved to Montreal, she changed her surname; initially Dave kept his birth father's name. The situation, he said, was alienating.

> Being from a divorced family in 1960 in suburban Montreal was not a common thing. And when we moved here, I had a different name than my mother and her husband. All of those things were like unusual at that time and people definitely looked at it as if there was something wrong. And in grade 5, I finally went to the teacher and said could you just call me Smith from now on and forget about Standinfeldt? Just call me Smith. And she said sure. And that's how it happened, actually. From then on, my school records were changed to Smith.

Dave experienced exclusion by virtue of his parents being divorced and his classmates' confusion about his last name being different from his mother's. He felt that he "stood out" during these initial years in Montreal. The experience taught him how it felt to be excluded and to feel different from others.

Debra identified herself as belonging to a visible minority, since her parents were Chinese immigrants. Her parents did everything they could to ensure that the family fit in – so much so that Debra did not learn much about her own culture. As she explained,

> I never knew – I am Chinese. I never knew Chinese New Year existed my entire life growing up until I came to university down in Southern Ontario. Like, what is this holiday everyone is recognizing? My parents never recognized it. Not because it wasn't important, [it was] because they tried so hard for us to fit into everything else that they did all of the cultures and the customs and traditions of that city.

Debra witnessed her parents striving to be included in society to the exclusion of their own culture. From their perspective, there was no way to be both culturally unique and accepted in Canadian culture. For Debra, this taught her the importance of recognizing, understanding, and celebrating other cultures. That way, families do not feel the brunt of an either/or decision when it comes to preserving their cultural heritage in Canada.

Witnessing her sister struggle academically at school, Debra gained another perspective on exclusion. She became frustrated with the cookie-cutter approach teachers took toward struggling students.

> You know what? No matter how many times you are going to teach it, as long as you teach it the same way, this child is not going to get it. They are not getting it. So we have to do something that's different.

Debra believed that a variety of teaching methods were needed to meet her sister's academic needs, and she was frustrated that her sister's learning needs were not considered. That has motivated her, as a principal, to ensure that all students' learning needs are met in the classroom.

Anna identified her experiences growing up as an only child with a father who was a blue-collar worker and a mother who was a secretary to illustrate exclusion. She experienced verbal bullying from her father at home and from peers at school. As she stated,

> I didn't have a lot of opportunities that other kids would have had. And I had to kind of look for the experiences, as opposed to having them handed to me. I look at the opportunities my children have and the things that I can provide for them, which leads to those kinds of leadership opportunities. I didn't really have that, so I had to kind of go searching and looking for them.

Anna realized early in her life that she would have to persevere in seeking out opportunities for herself. These experiences made her more empathetic toward people who were excluded, and she is able to relate better to them now. As well, her early life experiences have made her a fierce proponent of breaking down patterns of exclusion that affect her students and their families.

Susan highlighted a number of experiences that led her to become a strong advocate for inclusion. She was an only child, and her mother was very ill with ulcerative colitis throughout most of her childhood. Dealing with this illness, Susan felt very isolated from her peers. "There were a lot of public ramifications of her [mother's] illness," she told me. "And so, I guess, there was a connection for me in terms of equality going way back, probably to when she was very ill and all of those years." Her family's situation was compounded by her father's financial difficulties. As Susan explained,

> My dad had a bakery, and they went bankrupt when I was in first grade. And we had to go into hiding. And so there was, I guess, that whole socioeconomic equity. There was the religious equity. I'm Jewish and my [father] he changed his family name to Jones because his father was a baker and they moved around quite a bit. And he experienced a lot of religious prejudice.

Susan's family went through self-imposed exclusion from others due to their financial problems; they endured discrimination because they were Jewish. Through these experiences, Susan learned to identify and understand other people's exclusion. These early life experiences also reinforced her belief that everyone is important and should be honoured and validated.

Role models

Several principals I spoke to cited people who had served as role models of inclusion for them. These role models provided the principals in my study with concrete experiences that were inclusive in nature. Some of these role models also fought for the inclusion of all people.

Nigel identified his father as his role model. His father was a Marxist and a member of the Communist party in England, where his family lived. "My siblings and I had a politically engaged and politically active upbringing," he told me. These discussions with his father helped Nigel to understand that the class structure was a very active and powerful barrier for many people.

Karen also cited her father as a role model. When she was seven years old, she moved with her family to Connecticut. This was during the Kennedy-Nixon years, the time of the civil rights movement in the United States. Her father was looking to purchase a house. As Karen remembered,

> When he sat down to sign the contracts, he noticed at the bottom of the contract it asked him to sign to agree that he would never sell the house to a black, a Hispanic or a Jewish person. And he was shocked, and we had come from Canada so this, you know – he was shocked. And he refused to do that. And, of course, there was a lot of pressure from my stepmother, for one, to buy it. And from the people in the company that had hired him to work there because it was just – it was pushed as, "Well, it's just common practice. I mean, if you want to live in this nice neighbourhood here, it's just, you know, just do it. It's just what you do."

Karen witnessed fiery conversations in which her stepmother pressured her father to sign the contract, but in the end he refused. In later years, her father told her that the decision was clear cut: "I'm not going to be part of doing something like that." She learned the importance of fighting against exclusion from her father.

Kristin stated that her mother was her main role model for inclusion. Her parents were both idealistic, but her mother was the more powerful influence. She remembered her mother as

> a strong, if not screaming, feminist, which was pretty unheard of. And my father, although appearing to be quite traditional, married my mother. And he had some traditional sides to him, but he had no sense that women or females shouldn't be engaged intellectually. And so that was just part of our household, and I was raised, my mother certainly raised me, to fight the system.

Kristin's mother provided her with the incentive to fight the system, her father supported her by believing that females should be part of all intellectual discussions and decision-making. Today Kristin fights the system, much like her mother did, but finds it very tiring and difficult.

Dave grew up in a family where progressive politics were discussed and debated each night at the dinner table. His grandparents had left Europe in the early 1900s and still had contact with family in Poland and Austria. During World War II, many of their family were killed in concentration camps. As Dave elaborated,

> The Holocaust played a role in terms of how I grew up thinking: that such a thing should never be able to happen again. And that sort of leads you – it doesn't lead everybody and certainly the Holocaust leads people to some really reactionary politics, too – but in our case, it led us to [radical politics]. My grandfather was, when they came from Austria, he was a cigar box maker in New York and became very involved in the union and was part of the Socialist Party. And my mother has memories of him making speeches on soapboxes on corners and the police coming and him grabbing her and grabbing the soapbox and running down the street.

Dave learned from his grandparents and his parents how to participate in progressive actions to fight for social justice. He also learned the importance of advocating for one's beliefs.

Peter, a Catholic principal working in a Catholic elementary school, said Jesus was his role model. The students in his school shared a commitment to Catholic education, and this commonality, in Peter's opinion, supported the inclusion of all students. He mentioned how the Bible describes Jesus as working with the ostracized and marginalized to bring them into society. Peter told me that,

> He [Jesus] went up against [... the] evil [of the] Roman Empire and fought against those who were rich, and [tried to end] religious persecution. I mean without going throughout the entire history books, He [Jesus] was the quintessential model for inclusion.

Peter said that he uses Jesus' teachings to ensure that students, no matter who they are or where they come from, are included in the school.

Experiences as a Student

Some of the principals identified experiences as elementary, secondary or university students that influenced their understanding of and commitment to inclusion.

Nigel remembered that the education he received in England was often given by disinterested teachers. Moreover, there were many beatings in the schools, and there was no expectation that students from working-class backgrounds would finish high school. He added,

> I had constant messages from teachers. Constant messages from teachers that were given, which were basically, "You lot are a piece of crap. You lot are pieces of crap and you're going nowhere and you're nobodies." Really, that was what we were told, very, very clearly. I was once told by a teacher – I was twelve 'cause you go to high school at eleven in England – so I'm twelve, doing this needlework thing in domestic science and I must admit, I hadn't sewn before. I'm trying to sew and the teacher said, "Well, that's terrible." And I said, "Well, I've never done this before and I'm not very good at this." She said, "Well, what are you good at? Are you good at anything? I can't think of anything that you're good at." That was the – and that was a message, I thought, "Wow, what a bitch." You know, that stood out pretty clearly to me.

Because of his socioeconomic status, Nigel was not expected to do well at school or to continue beyond high school. But he persisted with his education and started university. Nigel remembered that during his initial lecture at university the professor said,

> "You're all middle class in here." And he said, "Oh, I know some of you are now looking at me thinking you're not middle class, you're working class. But your parents had middle-class values in order for you to be here." I remember thinking, "Fuck off." No, I mean, just that constant message, you know, "You got here so you're like us. If you work on your accent and you, you know, play with things and you kind of, you know, refine your manners you can actually be just like the rest of us."

Nigel found that the same exclusionary attitudes toward the working-class students continued throughout his time at university.

Todd was a good student and athlete who came from a middle-class family. But as a gay male who had not come out to others in high school in the 1970s, he felt the pain of hearing jokes or disparaging remarks from others about homosexuality. As Todd explained,

> I felt that, if there were sissy jokes, for instance, then I internalized those and felt okay, well, those are directed towards me. Or when I hung out with my best friends, who just happened to be the girls, there was that sort of insinuation as well, and that sort of also wove its way into things.

Todd had to keep his sexual orientation a secret for fear of further exclusion and condemnation. This experience reinforced his later determination to include all people.

Debra remembered being called racist names by teachers and classmates. She never thought to complain because, as she contended, "That's the way it was, because it was always happening." Debra realized years later exactly what had happened to her and how pervasive racism was in the school system.

Peter was born in Malta and came to North America when he was six. Even though he is now in his early forties, he still remembers his grade one year,

> not speaking a word of English, and walking into class and having kids taunt. I remember [it] vividly. Also, the kids in my class were white Anglo-Saxon, spoke the language. [There] weren't too many other kids in the same boat as me, so it became pretty evident that, because I was different in many levels, I wasn't accepted. That caused a bit of grief for quite a bit of time.

Peter stated that this experience taught him the importance of ensuring that all children feel welcomed and accepted at his school.

Experiences as an Educator

Some of the principals identified positive or negative experiences as educators that had shaped their approach and commitment to inclusion. These examples served as evidence that significant motivating experiences can occur at any stage of a life or of an educational career.

Nigel, as a teacher, learned a lot about inclusion from two principals he worked for. Both principals were African-Canadian and committed to social justice. As Nigel elaborated,

> One was a principal... [who] believed that the problem with our system is that, you know, we don't have high academic expectations of black kids. So we better have them. And her way of – her idea of an anti-racist education was to make those kids come out the door academically successful. That was her picture of anti-racism. The other person who became equity coordinator for the board I was with at the time before merger – and he – his focus was on a sense of belonging for all kids. So feeling a part of the school community, that they were – value who you are but you're also – we're all also members of this community, too, and building that sense of inclusion in the community in that sense.

The first principal wanted high expectations to apply to all students, and the second principal placed great emphasis on building a "community" within the school. Nigel said that both experiences have helped him practice inclusion as an elementary principal.

Karen spent four years teaching in Cree villages in northern Ontario, where she witnessed how the community made decisions together and shared information. The band council and the teachers worked together to submit a letter to the Department of Indian Affairs and Northern Development requesting a change to the school calendar for their community. The newly proposed calendar permitted families to go out together at the freeze-up and break-up of ice for the goose-hunting seasons. Goose hunting was a traditional activity in the community. Karen remembered receiving a response back from the government that stated, "School begins September

1st, ends June 30th." She understood how exclusionary the government's response was to this community; the community's needs, history and culture were not being acknowledged. Even though the government excluded their voices from the decision-making process, the Cree band council meetings were very welcoming and inclusive. As Karen explained,

> Band council meetings included everybody in the village. I mean, everybody went. And everybody who wanted to speak spoke. So I learned a lot about inclusion by going to those band council meetings, too, come to think of it. Because anyone who wanted to speak had a voice. They weren't run by Robert's Rules of Order. There was a lot of storytelling. I learned a lot about holistic thinking there. You know, sometimes when a question was asked, the response would be a story that, at first, you would think had absolutely nothing to do with what was asked. But by the time they were finished, it was, like, "Oh, my goodness, that just captured the whole thing."

Karen witnessed how community members' ideas and insights were included in the decision-making process; everyone understood they had the opportunity to participate. She experienced the practice of inclusion in a large setting with many different people who did not hold similar opinions.

In Kristin's initial years as an elementary principal, she discovered that there were certain expectations placed on a female administrator. She explained,

> As a female principal who moved very fast into administration, and as a female principal some would see as probably at least "acceptable" in terms of physical attributes, there's a package that they [other members of the school community] are expecting, and then when there is the roll-out of this challenge of the system, and I expect an intellectual relationship, that seems to create problems for people…So as long as I am a somewhat submissive – and more than somewhat submissive some days – female, attractive, and I play that card, I will be included in many things, but if I challenge or if I use much of the intellectual component which I find interesting, that's seen as arrogant or that's seen

as inappropriate or that I don't know my place, and I find that very frustrating.

Even though she was a school principal, Kristin's intellectual challenges to the educational system were not always welcomed or appreciated because she was female. The members of the senior administration, both male and female, reacted in similarly negative fashion. These experiences made Kristin even more aware of the need to advocate for female administrators.

Tony remembered how excluded he felt as a beginning teacher in the system. He described the school decision-making environment as top-down and authoritarian, a system in which only the principal had input. He and the other teachers on staff did not question this type of administration at the time. As Tony stated,

> I always felt like, I don't care if it [the undisputed hierarchy of schools] works or not. I don't have a say in it. I mean, I was a university graduate, and I can't have a say in what's going on? That just felt ridiculous. So I think my own experience of not having any opportunity to have an ownership or involvement in the decision-making, even in those early days, made me realize that, no, people have to have a say. And if they don't have a say in it, you're never going to have an effective environment.

Tony's own experience of exclusion taught him the importance of including everyone in discussions and decision-making.

Anna gained valuable experience working as a special education consultant with different schools, some of which were located in very high-needs areas. She witnessed how students identified through the Identification, Placement, and Review Committee (IPRC) process were not always supported in the schools. She explained,

> Going into the different classrooms and observing, it was the teaching practices more than observing the kids. And you could see that – and it wasn't intentional. I don't think teachers intended to do that but it's easier. It's easier for [those students] to sit in the back of the room and just be at

their desk or look – because you're kind of, "I've got a curriculum to teach, so I've got to go through." And I would sit at a meeting and teachers would ask, "Do you mean I have permission to do this?" Absolutely. Or else this person or these two little guys sitting in your class are never going to be able to participate.

Teachers did not know how to include the special education students in learning opportunities. Rather than taking each student as an individual and tailoring the curriculum to his or her needs, they found it easier to follow the "manual" of teaching practice without questioning it. The result, as Anna saw, was a pervasive exclusion of special education students.

Susan began her teaching career in an inner-city school in New York City. She began working with a student named Carl who was repeating grade one. Carl taught her a valuable lesson. She explained,

We used the Bank Street Reading Series. I gave him the book that we were all using. And, lo and behold, he became a terrible behavior problem. I think it was really a gift that he gave me, because I realized I wasn't meeting his needs. And then I began the search, really, to look for what else I could do. I went to lots of professional development, and I began, within the corridor of my school program, brain-based learning, multiple intelligences, cooperative learning, teaching to the level that the children were at, and so we took over a corridor of the school. The program became a model for the New York City Board of Education.

Susan considered this program a model of inclusion, because every child's academic and learning needs were met. She believed students could be included more effectively if supportive programs were in place. But with a subsequent budget crisis, this model program was cut, and she returned to teaching a class of thirty-five students.

The Power of Stories

Stories about the lives of school participants can be very effective teaching tools for growing inclusion. Deal and Peterson (2009) assert, "For some time, the role of stories in organizations has been marginalized by a pervasive fascination with logic and numbers" (74). While Deal and Peterson are more concerned with the transmission of a school culture through stories, however, I see the importance of stories as supports for getting to know our students, parents, and staff members. Maynes, Pierce, and Laslett (2008) posit that individuals and their actions are often placed in categories (race, gender, etcetera) that set them outside of the social world; they are understood only in reference to these clusters of categories (18). Personal stories and narratives, on the other hand, provide insight into people's lives. As Mayne, Pierce, and Laslett (2008) further write,

> Personal narrative analyses…offer insights from the point of view of narrators whose stories emerge from their lived experiences over time and in particular social, cultural, and historical settings. These analyses offer insights into human agency as seen from the inside out; as such they can bridge the analytic gap between outside positionalities and interior worlds, between the social and the individual (16).

All of the principals I spoke to had experiences of marginalization or exclusion that motivated them to seek inclusion in their schools. These experiences were so powerful that seeking inclusion became an intrinsic part of their identities. Many educators, however, especially those from privileged backgrounds, have not had similar experiences. This raises the question: How do I motivate my staff members to grow inclusion if they have not endured exclusion or marginalization themselves?

The answer is straightforward: as the principal, I must devote time to teaching my staff about inclusion and exclusion and the impact of these on the students in our school. Fullan (2011) posits,

> …exhorting people to have greater moral commitment is often less effective than helping them get new experiences that activate their moral purpose. The establishment of new practices and experiences galvanizes passion (23)

Furthermore, the learning my staff and I undertake must have significant experiential and practical components. Simply giving staff members written information will not cut it; they need to experience success at using practices and strategies that flow from the goal of growing inclusion.

In the next chapter, I outline strategies for teaching staff members about inclusion while ensuring that they, too, are included in the school.

———•—•——

CHAPTER 4

Growing Inclusion with Teachers

> Principals have little direct contact with students and certainly not enough to transmit the subtleties of an institution's culture and beliefs. If a school is to have a powerful ethos, it is the teachers who must communicate it, embody it, and transmit it. Indeed, teachers are the one stable influence on a culture. (Cohen 2002, 532).

AS PRINCIPALS, WE INFLUENCE SCHOOL CULTURE by working with and through teachers. Since it is teachers who have the greatest impact on students, growing inclusion in schools demands that they be the key players in the process. So the majority of practices and strategies vital to growing inclusion in schools pertain to teachers, and their work.

1) Teaching Teachers about Inclusion

Teaching your staff about inclusion is the most important step in the process, since building staff capacity in this area will affect both the short-term and the long-term application of inclusive practices in your school. As principal, you do not need to be the expert here, or the only resource. Your role instead is to facilitate the learning that takes place about inclusion, making use of as many human and material resources as you can. In my current school, there are many staff members who are much more well-versed than I with regard to understanding Aboriginal people's history of exclusion and oppression. I am still learning too. But while you need not be the expert, as your school's principal you must be inclusion's fiercest proponent.

i) Expressing your personal values regarding inclusion. This strategy involves the principal being explicit to staff members about his or her feelings about inclusion. You can use both formal and informal opportunities to share your beliefs, either verbally or as written communication. This is a direct strategy that sometimes involves addressing the issues in very public ways.

Karen acknowledged that staff members in her school knew how she felt about inclusion because she "wore [her] feelings on her sleeves." She cited the example of a disparity in the number of field trips for different student populations at one school. When she arrived at the school as principal, she learned that the extended French students, many of whom came from affluent families, had greater opportunities to go on field trips than the poorer English program students did. Karen was new to the school, and she remembered her first staff meeting.

> I was fairly dogmatic and unilateral about that. I said, if field trips are going to be offered for a grade, they'll be made available to the neighbourhood classes as well as extended French. And we'll just have to find fundraising ways to accommodate that. And if everybody can't go, then that trip won't happen.

In this example, Karen did not open the discussion up to staff. She used her positional power to state to staff members that inclusion was going to happen. In Karen's view, there are instances where principals have to be very clear and exact about how they feel. Even though she was new to the school, she demonstrated her personal values on inclusion when she encountered a traditional exclusionary practice. This situation was especially challenging because this practice had been in place for several years prior to her arrival.

Brent told me how important it was for him, as principal, to communicate what he believed in during the first staff meeting at each school. At that meeting, staff members learned that he valued their participation in all aspects of school life and decision-making.

Allan described to me how he advocated for the special education students in his school. In one situation, he insisted that developmentally disabled students be included in the school assemblies. Allan told staff members,

> We've got an assembly coming up. That D.D. [developmentally disabled] class is gonna be a part of this assembly. If they're not a part of it they're gonna sit in the front row and be right there. I don't care how much noise that autistic kid is making. What are you doing when you see kids in your class being excluded to make sure that they're not the last person picked in baseball? To make sure that they're not always on that, you know, history project group that's gonna get a low mark?

Allan's staff members understood from his words and his actions that he expected all students to be included in and around the school. He was also specific about what he wanted. This meant that inclusion went beyond talk at staff meetings and was manifested in concrete practice.

Debra remembers arriving at her new school as principal and listening to staff members complain about both parents and students. Being new to the school, she learned quickly that many staff members held negative views of the students' parents and guardians. She elaborated,

> I'd say maybe half my staff believed that parents are just lazy, and the children are just lazy and not interested. And…we really got into talking to the parents. And one of the things I have mandated for every staff member is by the end of the second week of school, every parent has to be contacted. I don't care by phone, in person. You go out and just meet them as they are dropping off the children. Every parent has to be contacted. And then every parent has to be contacted through the agendas or classroom newsletters.

Debra believed strongly that staff members must connect with and include their students' parents; she knew that she had to confront these negative perceptions. In this instance, she did not garner opinions or seek consensus from staff members. She stated exactly what she wanted to happen.

ii) Sharing your personal views on leadership. As outlined, it is crucial to communicate your personal views on inclusion to staff members, and the same holds true for your views on leadership. How do you define leadership in your school, and what does this look like in daily practice? Is your conception of leadership consistent with your views on inclusion?

A number of principals I spoke to highlighted the importance of devoting time to thinking about leadership and then communicating their ideas to staff members. Karen remembers speaking during an early staff meeting about some of the things she valued. At this meeting, she and her staff were deciding what they wanted to focus on for the year. She recalled,

> there were the things that were mandated by the board. But we just had different ways of handling it. I think for a lot of teachers it was kind of a relief for them to hear me say that test scores are not going to be the main focus of what we do. I mean, literacy's important. Who's going to argue that literacy opens up worlds for children? But there were lots of ways of going at that.

Karen encouraged staff members to participate in decision-making for the school year, even though their school's priorities were clearly outlined by the school board. She suggested there were ways to move away from the school board's focus toward what staff members believed their students needed. In this way, staff members learned that their voices were important, and were encouraged to consider that there was more to student success than simply test-score results.

John stated that two levels of leadership were vital in his school. First, a structure for inclusion needed to be developed, so that inclusion could become part of the school culture. Staff leadership was the important second level. John told me,

> there is also looking at where individual staff or a team of staff are, in terms of leadership development. I think one thing that we learn as principals through our advocating for inclusion is [that we have] to provide opportunities for people to lead successfully. And we don't always have a staff that are ready for that type of leadership.

In order to provide successful leadership development for staff members, John said, development needed to be aligned with his staff members' areas of expertise. The other critical part of his conception was that inclusion must become part of the daily "happenings" at his school.

Brent indicated his belief in a shared-leadership model rather than the single-leadership models he disdained. As he elaborated,

> Most of our leadership models are singular, male, Messianic-type of leadership models. And they're highly inappropriate and ineffective, I think, because they create a significant amount of collateral damage in the decisions that they make. The great leader makes great decisions in their own eyes, but in everyone else's eyes often there's collateral damage emotionally, professionally, and personally that happens. Kind of all-for-one, one-for-all type of approach where we really work together to make decisions, we commit to them. And then we follow them through, even if there's some difficult things that we need to deal with. And so I'm always encouraging staff members to have a voice. I try to really encourage as many people as possible to have input into decisions, given time, and, I guess, the need for the decision to be made.

Because Brent believed the "singular leadership" model tended to damage relationships within the school, he sought input from others prior to making most decisions.

Dave reminisced about the staffing committees from years past that included both staff members and parents. Unlike similar committees today, these groups had the power to make decisions. Currently, staffing committees are consultative in nature, with the principal retaining the positional power to make the final decision. Dave believed very strongly in involving all concerned people in all parts of the decision-making process. He described how he ensured this:

> I would always do a draft of whatever that plan was, and it was a continuation from the year before in many ways, but then the draft would go out to people. They would give

feedback. We would meet and talk about it, and then the staffing committee would really talk about it in great detail in terms of what were things that they thought were important to focus on, in terms of, like, staffing issues, so that what the program was [was] reflected in the staffing.

According to Dave, if staff members believe "that their voice and their practice is real and valued, people are happy to participate."

Anna differentiated between providing opportunities for stakeholders to participate and providing experiences for stakeholders. Her conception of leadership involved the principal clearly knowing the needs of all participants, particularly the students. She explained the distinction by saying,

> I don't want to provide opportunities, because opportunities can be taken or not taken. So I'm thinking, for me, it's providing all the stakeholders with experiences that allow full participation in all aspects of school life. They need to be – you can give anybody an opportunity, but whether they take it or not is the difference. To me, it's providing them with those experiences so that they do participate in helping students to participate academically, socially, emotionally.

Susan believed that the leadership team should be open to anyone who wanted to participate. In her mind, leadership did not reside in a single person but within groups of people. The leadership team in her school, she said, was,

> inclusive for everyone who wants to come. So everyone's invited. The community is invited. Not students, because it's not at a student level. The chairs come because they feel they have to. But certainly other people do come, as well. And it's always open. So people can come when they so choose. I purposely don't make it so that it's exclusive of anyone.

At Susan's school, there was flexibility for staff members, parents, and community members to participate when they wanted: they could join the leadership team at any time. By having regular meetings that anyone could attend, she attempted to make this inclusive practice part of the daily fabric of the school.

Peter used inclusive and shared-leadership models to structure his school's operations. He was passionate about ensuring that there was a lot of participation in all aspects of decision-making in the school. "Committees basically run most of the items in the school," he said. These committees also had the power to make decisions.

Craig used the YMCA triangle symbol to illustrate how students' needs should be met. He continually made reference to this symbol throughout the school year and, he told me, communicated this vision to staff members. He noted that the triangle

> stands for the "whole student," we call it. The prophecy academic, the left-hand side is, you look at it, it's a social, most essentially it touched your heart. The right side is physical and [a] social flexure radar. So to me that's the old takeoff from the YMCA: The mind, the body and the soul. [...] That's the image I try to drive at the people because I'm learning more and more in implementing anything or trying [to get] people to understand. You can do the superficial, you can set up the programs, but you really got to get to the core. So, to me the core is [that] we go back to our staff members. We go back to starting with their philosophy of education and every year I asked my staff, "What's your philosophy education?" Let's take turns to [hear] it because every teacher has one, I mean that's part of your expectation, that was your account with the master triangle, and how does it match the things you do? And not just the triangle but all that [...] goes into our professional learning community teams.

Craig discussed the triangle symbolism with staff members so that there would be a shared understanding of the emphasis on supporting the whole student, not just the student's academic performance. He provided opportunities for staff members to relate their own beliefs on education to this leadership paradigm. He encouraged ongoing reflection from all staff members as to how their actions and words connected to these core commitments.

iii) Discussing inclusion with your staff. Several principals stated that they discussed the concept and practice of inclusion with their staff members. These discussions occurred both during formal meetings – such as staff meetings or on P.A. days – and during the many informal conversations that took place each day.

As the principal of a school with a significant number of Aboriginal students and several Aboriginal teachers, I dedicate a portion of each staff meeting to the discussion of Aboriginal cultures, histories, and knowledge bases. Aboriginal staff members use the meeting to educate others on how better to support students; all staff are encouraged to ensure that our school reflects and celebrates Aboriginal culture. Each presentation lasts no more than ten minutes of a sixty-minute meeting, but it serves as a structured practice of understanding our students and their families. As a whole staff, we then talk about how we could incorporate these new learnings into our teaching and our classroom environments. I want to keep the message and focus constant throughout the year.

As principal of her school, Nina used staff meetings to discuss how her students were marginalized in society. Staff members continued to talk about the needs of students and the community throughout the school year. Nina also used a school-community committee, on which many staff members sat, to share information and discuss inclusion.

Nigel used an equity audit to begin the discussion of inclusion with his staff. He, his staff, and the parents of his students participated in an examination of his school's practices as they related to both equity and inclusion. Because he and his staff wanted their school improvement plan to focus on equity, they gathered information using a survey that was given to all stakeholders. The equity audit was the first that the school had ever had. Because of this, and the comprehensive nature of the audit, the process took almost a year.

Some principals do informal equity audits. In the example cited earlier, Karen opened discussion about a school tradition to highlight the overarching need for inclusion in the school's environment. Karen did not believe that students in the school's English stream were being treated equitably. The issue over the field trips helped to open discussion on how to include all students in the school. Karen encountered much resistance since the practice was entrenched, and it took ongoing discussions with staff members to make that structural change in the school.

In my second year as principal of a generational poor school (issues of poverty having an impact on generations of families) whose students were predominantly white, I used a portion of time in each staff meeting to discuss inclusion. Our discussions focussed initially on general issues of inclusion, then slowly became more specific and applicable to our students' lives. A particular focus for us that year was on how successfully we were including and empowering our female students, since a significant number of them did not go on to complete secondary school. I met with several female teachers who shared a passion for issues of inclusion and equity; they told us during a staff meeting that in high school each of them had been dissuaded from pursuing any particular subject or skill because they were "pretty and were going to get married anyways." After they shared their experiences, we discussed as a staff how we could support our students. Using staff members' life experiences is an effective method of beginning the discussion of inclusion and exclusion in your school.

As the principal of a school in a socially disadvantaged neighbourhood, Debra talked with her staff members about the instability and terror that sometimes lurked in students' lives. Not all staff members, she said, understood the reality of their students' home lives. She explained further:

> They hear me saying it, but I don't believe all of them truly understand. The ones who truly understand are the ones who walk our kids home after tutoring sessions. The ones who understand are the ones who really understand the kids and know that the children are falling asleep in class because they are up all night wondering what gunfire was happening out in the community.

Debra knew that more dialogue was needed to help her staff better understand the students' needs.

Tony, another principal, devoted time at meetings to sharing information about certain students' lives, so that teachers could understand some of the factors involved in the behaviour of those students. He ensured that classroom teachers were aware of some of the challenges that their students were facing socially, emotionally, and academically.

Kristin recalled an assembly at which a number of students demonstrated their writing ability in front of the whole school, and almost all them were white, female, and high achievers academically. At the next staff meeting, she began a discussion about this.

> I kinda opened the conversation. I didn't say what I saw – I waited to see if anyone else had seen what I saw. Sure enough, one teacher said, "Well, you know, they were all white and, um, this is a pretty multicultural school…." And so we had a little bit of a conversation about that and then I said, "Well, you know the other thing that I noticed that was every one of the kids that read really could write, and that meant that there was quite a group of kids, despite our extremely high test scores, that weren't up there, because they're maybe not quite as strong."

After Kristin had introduced the topic and shared her opinion, other staff members joined in and plans were made for the next assembly to be based on themes from their discussion. The next writing assembly was far more representative of the student population.

iv) Sharing educational resources about inclusion. This practice involves providing staff members with information that supports their ongoing learning about inclusion and exclusion. Some examples of resources are scholarly articles, books, magazine and newspaper articles, and visual presentations.

Brent provided his staff members with educational articles during staff meetings and led discussions on the topics these raised. While he employed a democratic approach to staff meetings, he ensured that his staff members were regularly reading literature about issues of equity and social justice so that they became more self-aware in their practice as teachers, particularly in terms of their engrained patterns of thought. He used the staff meetings to "extend" and "broaden" his staff members' understandings of the various topics.

Dave led a staff book club at school to help expand the concept of equity. He remarked that the book club was

> voluntary, but two-thirds of the staff would be a part of the book club. They got the book for free and dinner. But those books were always selected to be books that challenge people's thinking around issues of equity. There would be a little committee of people who would sort of organize the group and make up a selection of a few books that we would then bring to the whole group.

The book club get-togethers provided staff members with excellent opportunities to discuss issues relevant to what they were doing in the school. They connected what they were reading with their own experiences. As principal, Dave purchased the books, paid for dinner, and supported the initial start-up. Soon a committee was making the decisions about which books would be chosen. Through its work, the committee developed a much more comprehensive understanding of issues related to equity and social justice.

v) Inviting guest speakers to share insights on inclusion. Using guest speakers to support inclusion is a practical and effective strategy to complement in-school staff learning. If chosen well, speakers can provide great insight into, and instil deeper comprehension of the lives, experiences and worldviews of a diverse student population.

At my school, on a professional development day, I brought in a university professor to work with us on deficit thinking and issues of equity. My hope was that some of the prevailing attitudes among staff members would be challenged, and that everyone would emerge with a better understanding of how the educational and social systems work to marginalize certain groups and individuals. The professor had a confrontational approach and style of delivery, but staff members felt comfortable speaking up and even disagreeing with the professor. This was largely because we had been discussing inclusion and equity ourselves for many months at staff meetings, at grade team meetings, and on professional development and activity days.

Debra invited a woman from Somalia to a staff meeting to educate staff members on some of the children's experiences and how those could possibly explain certain behaviours in the school. The discussion was crucial to staff members better understanding the students they were serving. Debra and other principals also worked together to promote knowledge of inclusion through visits to different places of worship. As she explained,

> The principals invite one staff member with them. We hire a bus, and we go to three different [religious organizations]. [...] This last one I went to was a Pentecostal church, a Sikh temple, and a synagogue. And we sit there, and we listen to the religious leaders talk about what is important and how it connects to the education.

Principals and teachers learned together on these outings, sharing the experience with educators from other schools. The principal and staff member would then return to their own school and share their experiences. Having a teacher from each school participate helped to ensure that the message to staff members would not be viewed as simply coming from the principal, that is from the top down.

Tony used both presentations by staff members and by outside speakers to spark group discussion about inclusion in the school. He explained,

> staff meetings were basically presentations. So I would have the social worker come in and do a presentation, I would have the psychologist, I would have staff do presentations on special ed. support service, do presentations on our kids and their needs and how best to service them. And then I had speakers come in. I had a couple of speakers from the black community who came in, and really one of them really provoked the staff.

The presenter Tony mentioned managed to jolt his staff by outlining how white educators unwittingly discriminate against black students. The speaker confronted staff members on their beliefs and assumptions. As a result, staff members were forced to reflect on their own practices, their actions and their behaviour toward all students. For weeks afterward, Tony told me, staff members continued to discuss the content of the presentation. The type of professional development in his school varied depending on the subject matter; some learning experiences were meant to challenge staff members.

vi) Improving pedagogical practice to support student learning. Supporting students in making significant academic progress is also critical to growing inclusion. Ongoing professional development that aligns with staff needs and student learning data is paramount.

Nigel used critical literacy and a critical-focus model for his whole staff to examine pedagogical practice and resources at his school. This was one of the major foci for the year. As he explained,

> You know that there are kids who don't see themselves reflected in what we do.[...] I don't like the idea in some ways of African Heritage Month. I don't like the idea of celebrations because I think they can certainly trivialize what we do and what we're trying to do. But what I wanted to do was try to find ways to integrate this into the curriculum far more effectively than doing a few little shows. I really wanted it to become whatever it is we're doing. Let's look at the contributions of black people. And then let's build on that.

Nigel provided staff members with a critical lens through which to examine the curriculum; they examined history and social studies texts for bias. This critical lens also helped staff members to spot omissions in the curriculum and explore ways to address them. As a result, the curriculum quickly became more representative of the student population.

A main focus at Todd's school was on meeting the academic needs of at-risk students. This was achieved through professional development on differentiated instruction combined with in-servicing on equity and diversity issues. On the subject of professional development, Todd stated,

> I try not to be the one delivering the P.D. I think that – I'm the one doing the staff meeting and so I find that I'd much rather have, you know, a teacher colleague and, or say, someone from a department to be able to come in and provide P.D. for the staff. Then, that way, they're a teacher colleague; the teachers have a tendency to pay a little more attention to them. They're getting the message from a colleague as opposed – it doesn't come across as being top-down.

By involving many different educators in the delivery of professional development, Todd ensured that his staff members would be more receptive to what was being offered.

Anna and her staff members examined how the special education students in their school were being excluded academically in the classroom. She led the school's direction team, a collection of staff members who met to design a school improvement plan in terms of student achievement, and provided extensive support to staff members on how better to meet the academic needs of special education students. When special education students were discussed at team meetings, she ensured that staff members were provided with guidance and support in meeting the students' needs. She explained,

> Some of the MID [mild intellectual disability] students in there may have not had the experience and probably needed the visual on how to put it together, because orally, they can't quite follow the conversations. So those are the little things that I put together in those in-school meetings.

Anna emphasized to staff members that the strategies they developed had to be "doable for you, but also help the student." Staff members also knew that they were expected to apply these strategies in the classroom on an ongoing basis.

Susan told me that her entire staff was "Tribes trained." Tribes, a program used in schools to promote inclusion and community, helps ensure that all people are included and heard. Susan's school also used "We're Erasing Prejudice for Good," an anti-oppression curriculum resource, in all classrooms. To facilitate the use of this resource, she combined two important committees within the school: the equity and literacy committees. Susan explained further,

> They didn't have an equity committee before I came. So the equity committee and the literacy committee worked together. And our committees have a representative from each of the grade teams. So they can go back to the grade team [and communicate with all the teachers in the school]. They worked together and they did a professional development session on "We're Erasing Prejudice for Good" and linking it to equity.

Piggybacking the equity committee on the literacy committee's established structure and reputation within the school meant that all staff were immediately included in the conversation about equity. As well, combining the two committees allowed staff members to learn from one another in a collaborative manner rather than learning through a top-down, principal-directed conversation.

Peter told me his school used balanced literacy to ensure that all students had their academic needs met. Balanced literacy, which incorporates numerous pedagogical modalities, provided a stepping stone to a broader conversation about varying teaching strategies to appeal to as many learners as possible. Peter noted that too often teachers tend to teach in one way only, even though not all students learn in the same way. There was ongoing professional development at his school on differentiating instruction to help teachers meet students' diverse learning needs and bring more students into the process.

vii) Modeling inclusive behavior. This strategy is also known as "walking the talk" of inclusion. Modeling inclusive behaviour involves both verbal and nonverbal behaviour.

Nigel told me he ensured that the different staffing groups were included in all decisions. He also included special education assistants in the interviewing of teachers they would be working with, which surprised the educational assistants. All staff members understood that others were to be consulted and included. Nigel explained,

> You show your priorities through your actions. One of the
> things you do as a leader is you show that. I mean, you've
> got to model it. Show who you are and what you believe in
> by what you do.

Nigel understood that by involving others he demonstrated his own commitment to inclusion. All staff members, and particularly teachers, could see by his including educational assistants in the hiring process that he valued their input.

Kristin described how she modeled inclusive behaviour to her vice-principal, her staff members, and other parents by the way she interacted with people. She explained that on yard duty, for example,

> I will talk to the parents that look like me, and I'll enjoy
> that, but I am aware that I need to stretch out and make
> sure I am doing that with people that don't look like me.
> And, I think, I think if I were going to be there ten years,
> over time that might make a difference.

Kristin knew that not all staff members or parents interacted with one another on school property before and after school. She recognized that, as the principal, she needed to take the first step in changing that.

Brent noticed that sometimes staff members did not practice inclusion with one another. For example, teachers and educational assistants did not always include secretaries, custodial staff or child-care workers in staff activities or events. He explained,

> I will continually encourage staff to make the social events
> conform to a format, or a time, that might allow more of
> those people to be involved. And so wherever I can, I'm
> always looking for ways to respect people, acknowledge
> people and treat them with respect, personally, when I deal
> with them, as well.

Brent demonstrated his commitment to inclusion through his ongoing efforts to change these structures within the school.

Susan believed that a number of components contributed to how she modeled her behaviour toward others. As she elaborated,

> [Staff members] see, I think, that my values come through on a regular basis in terms of all the decisions that happen in the school. And through my support of them, in terms of them being successful, and in my work with teachers who have less capacity, and sending them for professional development and dialoguing with them and supporting them so that they feel better about themselves as teachers.

Matt communicated very clearly to his staff members the important principles that must be part of everyday practices within the school. After stating these important principles, he said,

> You have to act them out on a daily basis. And you have to use them in everyday situations so that you establish a pattern of acting upon a certain value, so that people start to associate that with you, and then associate that with the school, and then associate that with the kids.

Matt believed that staff members, parents, and students started to expect a certain pattern of behaviour at the school after they perceived consistent behaviour from the principal. He believed that, over time, staff members would begin to model these same inclusive behaviours with students.

Craig, like Matt, was very direct about his expectations of staff members pertaining to inclusion. He also knew how critical it was for him to model this inclusionary behaviour. As he explained,

> I've modeled those expectations [through] the way I dress, the way I walk around the school. I talk about being visible all the time, so I make sure I'm visible. So, it's hard to explain in ten words or something, [because it is] something you act on day to day. So I say I do it by my physical presence, I do it by the way I talk. I've been trained as a guidance counselor before [... I became a principal, so] I learned the power of active listening and I make sure I active listen to people. Probably the best skill I have ever learned from active listening is paraphrasing. So if I say I

> include you and respect you, then I use paraphrasing a lot
> in talking to kids, parents, anyone, because to me it demon-
> strates I'm trying to understand what you are saying.

Craig ensured that his interactions and dialogues with staff members, students, and parents were inclusive in nature. He listened to others and then paraphrased back to them to demonstrate that he understood their message. This role modeling was something he had to do each and every day; as a result, people began to connect these inclusive values and behaviours with him.

2) Including Staff Members in the School

Staff members will only "buy into" and embody inclusion if they, too, are included in the school. Growing inclusion will not work if teachers feel alienated or excluded; just like students, they must be "of" the school and not simply "in it." It is teachers who will continue the practices of inclusion long after you, as principal, have been transferred to another school. Staff members bring many different talents and experiences to the school, and they need to have the power to shape their work environment.

i) **Listening.** One of the most valuable practices for a principal is active listening: listening to understand. It is a strategy that should be used with all school participants, and one that is extremely important in supporting and understanding staff members. Sometimes staff members simply want a place to vent or to share their experiences after a particularly challenging day. Other times, however, they may need your support with a personal situation, be it a divorce, a health issue, or a challenging colleague, parent or student.

Effective listening skills, according to Nigel, start with something very basic: the principal ceasing to speak. Immediately, staff members will feel more comfortable sharing information. He explained,

> Stop talking and find out what they think. That's really the
> fundamental piece of any of this stuff. If you want to know
> what's going on, then you have to ask people, and you have
> to listen. It's not just that, but you have to give people a space
> and a format, and you have to make it non-threatening.

Nigel set up interviews to help him learn about his staff members' lives and interests. These gave him tremendous insight into the school's strengths and potential areas of growth. He understood that if he wanted to learn about the school, he needed to stop talking and begin listening.

Todd used a survey to gather information about his school, asking staff members, students, and parents about all aspects of school life. The survey provided him and his staff with information on how all stakeholders perceived the school. The results helped to identify the school's needs and also shone a light on students who were at risk.

John used a Stephen Covey strategy from *7 Habits of Highly Effective People*: "First seek to understand and then be understood" (Covey, 1990). He agreed with other principals that an inclusive environment requires the principal to seek information and listen. John explained,

> I do believe you have to listen twice as much as you talk. Like, what are the behaviors telling us? What are the interactions telling us? What is an apparent aloofness telling us about our school environment? I think that we have to observe twice as much as we listen[...] really watch what is going on there in a nonjudgmental fashion.

John made the essential point that the principal also needed to examine the interactions among people. He told me that observing the interactions at his school was an effective means of gathering information about inclusion: he learned who was interacting with whom and the context in which these interactions took place.

Kristin believed that listening to staff members was vital to understanding how they perceived the world. She made it clear, as principal, that she valued staff members' individual views. Kristin explained that, when dialoguing with a staff member, it was crucial to

> listen to their story, understand their story. Listen critically to their story, but remember that that story is being told by a person, and that's pretty important, very important, to understand that. They're not making it up; that's how they see it.

By listening carefully she would learn how that person saw or understood the world.

Anna made certain her staff members knew she was always available to them if they had a concern, a question or a problem. She explained,

> If they [staff members] have an issue with another staff member or an issue with a parent or whatever, we'll shut the door and we'll have a conversation. I may not be – and they know I don't have the answers. They know that. I will never, ever say that I know, because I don't. I don't know everything. But I'll listen, and oftentimes we'll try to come up with a solution together, or I'll ask more questions.

Anna understood that these conversations were vital in building positive relationships with staff members.

Debra used weekly meetings with staff members from all employee groups to gather information and learn about what staff members were feeling and saying. She told me that these meetings helped her to understand the "pulse" of the school.

ii) Encouraging ongoing dialogue. Ongoing dialogue entails sharing between or among people. It helps the principal to get to know staff members, and vice-versa. As with the other practices outlined here, dialogue must be part of the way the school does business throughout the year. By getting to know staff members, the principal is better able both to support them and to grow inclusion with them. Kristin was one principal who devoted time to getting to know her staff members.

> I try to spend time with them socially, which doesn't include going out Saturday night but might include going out Friday after work occasionally [...] By talking to them about matters [...] related to, you know, what to do about this child or that child. But not just brushing that aside, really seeking that, and then sometimes that propels them forward as well. Despite being a fairly introverted person, I know my staff. I know them quite well, and so people come in and tell me what is bothering them and what is going on in their lives.

The conversations Kristin had with her staff covered elements of both the school day and the staff members' personal lives. Staff members grew comfortable talking with her, and she learned how to support their professional development. They knew that she cared about them and their lives, inside and outside of school.

Tony also used chats with his staff members to learn more about them. From these conversations, he tried to determine their strengths and weaknesses. Part of the process for Tony involved providing opportunities for staff members that aligned with their strengths; by knowing his staff members, he was better able to support them. This was especially true for staff members who had been labeled as the "detractors," individuals who did not get involved in extra-curricular support activities in the school. Tony explained,

> You have to look at why is it that they are detracting. What is it? Their own life experiences and their own life situations might be such that they can't take part. They want to, but they can't. And if they want to and they can't, then the frustration builds in and sometimes a defense mechanism is to try to tear it down, because [they] can't be part of it. So you find a way to allow them to be part of it, or you simply recognize that "I understand your situation right now. You're a mother or a new father, or someone's ill at home, or you're having difficulty. It's okay. Don't worry about it, just do what you can."

Anna emphasized the importance of remembering the human element when working with staff members. She lamented that, with the emphasis on collective agreements, policies, and procedures, the human aspect of the job was often lost or blurred. To counteract this, Anna set aside time to meet with staff members to learn about their lives. She outlined her views:

> To me – and I don't want to sound like my job isn't important, it absolutely is – but it is a job and it is a career. However, it's not our whole life. And I think we need to kind of keep that in mind. So [I have] lots and lots and lots of informal meetings with staff, just to get to know who they are and what they're about. Because I think that way, too, you get

to know what they need help in, and when you're moving staff along, you need to know who you can push without a problem, and who you need to push, but also be able to provide a lot of support for.

By creating many opportunities to communicate with staff members, Anna was able to discern who was having difficulties or challenges in their personal lives. She placed great importance on supporting teachers by recognizing that teaching is only one part of each staff member's life. She communicated this by

> asking questions about their family life, about who they are as a person, what's important to them. I'll pop into the classroom [...] or in the staff room, say, "How's your mom? Is she doing okay? How was your trip?" Just those kinds of things. Or I had one staff member who went to the doctor, and I said, "Well, how did you make out?"

Because of these small, thoughtful comments and questions, staff members knew that Anna valued both their personal and their professional lives. By being personally accessible to her staff members and emphasizing her interest in their personal lives, Anna created an environment where it was clear she cared about them not just as employees, but as people.

Employing a similar strategy, Susan met with each staff member individually for thirty minutes when she first became principal to learn more about the school and its history. The key was that she learned about the school from individual perspectives. Staff members also had the opportunity to ask her questions during these meetings. The meetings provided an opportunity for all parties to get to know one another, and for Susan to communicate that she valued staff members' personal and professional lives.

Peter also met individually with staff members at a new school, as well as making many class visits to continue the communication. As he explained, he had

> a lot of conversations that involved supporting the staff... Whether it be with an angry parent or with a difficult kid [it was about] really showing them that you were on their

side, not just being their boss, but being a support for them. And eventually, over time, they see you as a resource, as opposed to someone just telling them what to do. That trust factor improves as well. So it took a lot of time, and we are not quite perfect yet.

Like many of the other principals, Peter ensured that his communication with staff was ongoing.

iii) Supporting staff members' personal and professional lives. As noted, ensuring that staff members feel supported both professionally and personally is vital. The human component can be overlooked, given the pressures on schools today. But the participants in my research shared a commitment to supporting their staff members in all aspects of their lives, and a genuine belief that this was a significant part of their role as principal.

I learned this early on. During my first year of teaching, I sat down with a seasoned teacher, Brian, who was nearing retirement. We were talking about Brian's experiences in a variety of schools, working with a number of administrators. Brian mentioned that one principal he admired most had always been there to support him personally. Brian remembered one instance when the school received a call that Brian's son was ill, and the principal came right down to the class and took over the class so that Brian could go get his son. This principal demanded a lot of Brian and the other staff members, Brian told me, but they all knew the principal would also support them personally and professionally.

Debra described being available to staff members by phone, in person and by email throughout the school year. If she could not speak with the person right away, she would do so at the earliest possible time. As she explained, her approach

> really opens the door to "we can call [on] you for anything." And quite often I get, […] as a principal you get a lot of calls outside of school issues. Family issues, personal issues, you hear it all. And that opens the door to communication for everything.

Staff members knew that Debra would respond to their needs and concerns throughout the year, including their personal issues. She placed priority on being available at all times.

As principals, we expect our staff members to go above and beyond their professional mandates to help students navigate their lives. We must do the same for staff members.

iv) Maintaining an open-door policy. This strategy involves the principal being available throughout the day to listen to and talk with staff members in a welcoming and inviting way. Nigel expressed the belief that his staff needed to feel comfortable discussing issues with him. He explained,

> You have to give people a space and a format, and you have to make it nonthreatening. And you have to make sure that people feel that they will be treated decently if they raise an issue, or they raise a concern, or they have a point of view to talk about, or whatever it may be. I think we have to create that.

Nigel stressed the need for creating a welcoming atmosphere so that staff members would not avoid discussing issues, particularly challenging ones. He remained respectful toward the staff member if the person raised a negative issue or was critical. Otherwise, Nigel said, staff members would remain silent.

Kristin told me that her door was virtually never closed; she made herself available to staff members at all times of the day. Anna also said how comfortable her staff members were about coming into her office and discussing issues. She believed that she modeled inclusive behaviour in this way. Again, her listening abilities were central. Her staff members knew that although Anna did not have all the answers, she was always willing to take the time to listen and to problem-solve.

Nina had a similar "open door policy." She explained why staff members came into her office to talk:

> I'm inviting, so I'm not a scary lady. When they come and they have a problem, I listen to it, and lots of times their

ideas are better than mine. And so they know that I will make change based on their ideas if I believe that's in their best interests.

The staff members at Nina's school had witnessed changes as a result of their input. As Nina acknowledged, many of their ideas were better than hers. Being a principal did not mean that she had access to absolute knowledge.

v) Hiring. Hiring is a key strategy for growing inclusion, and one that can generate huge gains relatively quickly. Getting the staff best suited to your school is paramount for both the short-term and the long-term success of inclusion. Each staff member you select brings skills and influences to the classroom and to others on staff. Through internal and external postings, principals can hire staff members who are passionate about inclusion. Depending on the size of your school, you could have three or four positions, or more, available each year through postings.

The interview process is an excellent tool to help identify future staff members who will be allies and advocates for inclusion in your school. An applicant's answers to the questions that the vice-principal and I ask during the interview, the thoroughness of the reference checks, and our own gut feelings are all part of the equation. Is it important that potential staff members employ sound, relevant pedagogical practices? Absolutely. Is it important that potential staff members demonstrate an understanding of the systemic biases, structures and inequities that limit opportunities for many, and are willing to fight against them? Of course. I always place more emphasis on staff members being passionate about supporting students holistically than I do on their simply being skilled in the technical aspects of instruction. My experience has taught me that improving the techniques of instruction through professional development is easier than changing or altering someone's worldview.

My questions during the interview involve three core areas: 1) instruction (knowledge of and experience with high-yield instructional strategies); 2) a commitment to issues of social justice (demonstrated by experiences in and/or outside of school) and 3) the ability to connect with other school participants and work collaboratively in a team. This third component is vital, because inclusion involves staff members, students, parents and community members working together.

Dave told me he used the hiring process to find teachers who would work well in that particular school's environment. He stated,

> Over the years, there were many times when we were able to hire people, and a big source I always used was [the] student teachers who had worked in this school and who I was able to observe.

Dave believed that teachers were the most important supports of inclusion in the school, so the hiring process was crucial. As he told me, "I always felt that the most important thing I ever did in any school was who I hired."

Debra sought to hire teachers who complemented the skills currently represented in the school. She explained,

> I hire people that have skills that I don't have, which makes the world a better place for us at school because we have all of these different experiences. They may not have had these experiences themselves personally, but they can certainly give me that insight of where the children are coming from.

When Debra hired a staff member who had experience as a child-and-youth worker, for example, the new staff member provided invaluable guidance to the administrators when it came to dealing with students of lower socioeconomic status. Debra also placed importance on staff members' interpersonal skills. She explained,

> "As long as you have the compassion, the understanding, the willingness to include – and inclusion is a big one – as long as they have that or the potential to learn that, everything else – curriculum [for instance] they can learn."

Debra placed great value on the human components of each new position, seeking candidates who would be proponents of inclusion.

Susan expressed her values in a diverse school community by deliberately hiring staff members to make the staff more culturally representative. In particular, she realized that her staff had to be more representative of the specific language needs of the community. A more culturally representative staff would help more parents and students feel included in the school.

vi) **Promoting individual leadership.** There are always opportunities within the school for staff members to assume leadership roles. In some instances a staff member will identify an opportunity, but in many instances the principal sees the opportunity and encourages the staff member to take it on. Encouraging participation in leadership roles outside of the classroom context is a valuable model for including everyone in the school. Staff members need opportunities to lead, along with the requisite power and control to shape the activity and its outcome. Nigel discussed the importance of providing space and support to develop teacher-leaders in the school. He sought out teachers who were looking for different leadership experiences, and then watched for ways to provide those experiences. By combining appropriate experiences with the skills and interests of particular teachers, Nigel ensured that many staff members were leading initiatives or areas within the school.

Todd placed staff members in crucial positions to provide professional development in the school. Teachers led many of the sessions, and other teachers were often more receptive to getting the message from a colleague.

Karen stated that even though, as principal, she was responsible for what went on in her school, "You [the principal] certainly don't have to be the person on the front lines for all sorts of things going on." She described a certain teacher who was instrumental in creating opportunities for students:

> There was one teacher in particular who was the catalyst for it. It was her idea and so I just did everything I could to throw support behind it. I invited her and a team of the students that she was working with to [...] present their ideas to school council. So it was coming from the students, too. And I also made time at a staff meeting for them to do the same.

Karen did not exert control over the team's ideas, and she looked for venues that would allow them to present these ideas to others. Staff members, parents, and community members witnessed this teacher and her team of students' leading an event at the school.

John indicated that he assessed individual staff members with regard to leadership potential. This principal, in his experience, needed to know where staff members were in terms of leadership development. As one example, John created an excellent leadership opportunity for his office administrator, who wanted to contribute to the school outside of her regular role. With John's support, the office administrator led a group of ESL students, who acted as tutors for other students.

Kristin noted that teachers organized and led many different activities in the school, including sports teams. She explained,

> We have a number of sports groups that [are] organized by teachers, and really, what is run by me is, "Is it okay to do this?" but not, "How do I organize it?" The teacher that does the ski club – she completely organizes a hundred kids, their parents, a group of teachers, the buses, and they go skiing six times [a year]. It is not once! And it is all done by a teacher who asks, "Can I tell this child that doesn't have the money that we'll pay for it?" [I say,] "Absolutely."

Kristine encouraged these various programs, allowing teachers to have control over many of the activities, and providing them with support if they needed it.

Dave highlighted how he had organized his staffing allocation to support the placement of a teacher who led community outreach initiatives. Through the staffing allocation, Dave found time on the weekly schedule for this staff member to lead the development of home and school connections. He explained,

> He [the teacher] became like a community leader in terms of the school being always everywhere: helping organize community events, bridging – he was responsible for student teachers, a lot of stuff. But he was also responsible for

supporting the parent council. So he would make sure that everybody who needed to be phoned was phoned the day of the council meeting to make sure they were there. He made sure about daycare and the food and whatever.

The teacher led several initiatives to build connections between home and school and took a very visible and important leadership position within the school. Dave had made certain first that the staff member was a good "fit" with the demands of the role and had the necessary skills to be successful.

Tony communicated with staff members about various leadership opportunities in the school, connecting these with staff members' skills and areas of interest. Staff members acted as facilitators with student groups and in one instance created, for instance, a Christian leadership group that did a lot of fundraising for schools in Jamaica and Trinidad. Tony explained,

> In the beginning there were a couple of key staff that were really on the same wave [or] path as I was. And they just jumped right in and wanted to do different things in that area. But there were also other staff who were very expert in other areas of school, like one particular person was a real whiz with computers. And so the opportunity to create a robotics program in the school was there. So there were people that had certain expertise and that, I think, appreciated the direction we were moving in. [They] wanted to be part of it, and jumped in, and helped promote it. Some of them weren't into leadership and just wanted to be part of what was going on and wanted to be able to use it on their portfolio.

As Tony pointed out, some staff members took leadership positions right away because they were excited about what was happening at the school.

Susan created an equity committee that included all the different stakeholders in her school. She attended meetings but did not the chair the committee; teachers took turns acting as chairperson instead, coordinating equity initiatives within the school.

Craig identified staff members who acted as "champions" of the different areas within his school. He also used the word "champions" in his daily discourse with others to identify these leaders and committee chairs. Craig tried to connect people's interests and talents with the different areas of need in the school. As he explained,

> Our champions literally run the school. So these are people that I call "champions," like in front of staff and everyone. They know [one teacher] is one of the major champions of our school as far as our setting up of professional learning communities. The other way I get people a voice is "money talks." In our school, our budget is very transparent, but our budget decisions [are not top-down]; people are given their money as teams to make their decision.

Each champion had the freedom to work collectively with other staff members in the same area and to make decisions that affected the whole school. In this way, most staff members had opportunities to shape their work environment. Craig also ensured that the champions met as a group, in a "Circle of Champions," to discuss school-wide issues and initiatives.

vii) Encouraging group or committee leadership. Group or committee leadership involves staff members sharing leadership.

Nigel created an equity committee in his school that provided staff members with opportunities to learn and to plan for inclusion. For example, the equity committee determined that they needed to weed the library of sexist, racist and otherwise inappropriate materials. They worked together after school hours to remove materials that did not align with their equity vision for the school.

Todd has also had an equity committee in place at his school for the past couple of years. He explained,

> If something comes by the equity committee that […] needs addressing, then that can be the avenue that we go. If there's something that the board has come out with, that indeed some information needs to be disseminated to staff, then I can address it that way. Or something that has happened

in our school that has come by the office, either through a parent or through a student, or through a staff member, that we need to address.

The equity committee at Todd's school responded to board initiatives and planned for their subsequent application; committee members would then share the information with other staff members. As well, the committee addressed concerns brought forth by any member of the school community. In this sense, the committee provided an outlet conduit through which parent and student concerns could be heard and discussed.

Brent recounted how the members of a special education committee in his school worked together to identify the diverse needs of special education students. He placed great importance on the committee's work to support students. He explained that the committee met regularly,

> involving all of our special education staff in regular meetings, usually every two weeks to three weeks throughout the school year; where the special ed. staff – and that would include the [special education centre teacher], if there's a centre teacher, core resource teachers, my English teachers, whatever – would all sit down together[...] We would leave a space of time to meet every two or three weeks. And we would discuss the needs of the kids; that I felt was really important. And allow voices at the table, even people that weren't directly involved in a student's case.

Brent mentioned that he received favourable feedback from staff members because they felt they had made a significant contribution through this structured process of helping students.

Dave remembered putting together the "organizing committee" at his school. There were no strict guidelines on who could attend these meetings, and the results of the meetings were presented later to the whole staff. He explained,

> We met once a week at lunch.[...] There were people who were automatically there because of their positions, but nobody was forced to be there. It was a place where people

could come together to talk about directions for the school, possible projects that we could work on, to really go into detail around issues that you would then bring to the staff meeting as a whole, to sort of work out the details. And it really was a place where first-year teachers could come and be a part of figuring out, really, what the school could look like, that would be different, and how we could make things better in the school.

The weekly meetings also provided opportunities for educational assistants and teachers to share ideas and develop solutions. The emphasis on informal interactions, in which everyone could discuss school-wide decisions, meant that new teachers were immediately integrated into an inclusive environment.

Allan mentioned that he rarely made unilateral decisions as principal. Most often, when a decision needed to be made, "a committee was struck, or it was raised at a staff meeting." Allan explained that people were given time to provide input to the committee. The vital point here is that staff members, for the majority of decisions, had time to consider and discuss the issue prior to presenting their views to the committee.

Tony mentioned the importance of two committees at his school. One committee was called the "continual school-improvement team." He chose some people to be involved with this team based on their individual talents, and then left it open for any other staff member to join. One particular staff member Tony chose for the team "had no bones at all about picking out what was wrong or what was going on." That ensured the committee would arrive at an honest understanding of what was happening in the school. Tony explained,

> I didn't limit the number [of people]. Now, there are problems with that, because sometimes there'd be ten, fifteen people sitting there. It's a little difficult to get something done. So then you start looking at dividing up tasks. But just moderate[ly sized] groups, and then each group does a task. It's easier to deal with.

Depending on these activities, the team met every two or three weeks. Tony did not always determine the agenda of the meetings. The second important committee Tony identified was the "LSSAC" or Local School Staffing Advisory Committee. The LSSAC was a contractual team that was supposed to provide input and recommendations to the principal on all decisions that were made. Tony, however, provided them with more power than that. He elaborated,

> Sometimes the decision that they were making wasn't the one I wanted. That's the way it goes. You [have] got to be willing, once you lay that out there, if the decision isn't the one you want, well, that's too bad. And we went with it. We went with the decision. Now, I would also provide them all of the parameters around the decision, based on board policies and legislation and so on, so sometimes a decision I couldn't do because you can't do it because the Ministry says we can't do this. And they were very good about [...] understanding that. But most of the time, the decisions were made by them.

Tony understood that to be effective, both of these committees needed the power to make decisions, not just to provide input.

Peter indicated that committees led and organized most of the activities at his school, rather than the principal simply creating the policy and the staff members following it. In one instance, staff members and students created the school's policy around bullying. As he explained,

> It used to be called "anti-bullying," which sort of rings a tone of reactive response to bullying prevention, which is of course preventive. So we put that in the hands of a committee. Instead of it being a top-down, hierarchical piece, we looked at the committee to decide how we were going to do things. I'll give you an example: they decided to survey the students on their feelings around bullying. So that was a pretty neat little piece, because it forced the staff to look at the opinions of the students. It empowered the staff to empower the students and created a culture of trust.

While Peter was part of the committee, he did not determine the direction or specific steps taken; committee members collectively made the decisions. That meant better "buy-in" to the policy, because staff members had helped create it.

viii) Promoting whole-school activities. This strategy involves all school participants working together toward a common purpose or goal. Whole school activities: 1) involve all school participants; 2) have a common focus on an issue of social justice, either internal or external to the school; 3) provide multiple opportunities for participants to work together; and 4) give school participants the power to create and shape the activity. Whole school activity complements a focus of learning in the school; it involves all members in the school, even those who are not "on board" yet.

John worked with staff members on the planning of a whole-school initiative. He explained,

> I think the most powerful way to get to a more inclusive school environment or leadership environment is to base it on an authentic school-wide initiative that we work through as a community, all stakeholders. And then, when we are [all] going through the planning process, that allows us to start to use the vocabulary right. So in essence it's no different than talking, than teaching a class. But then you begin to immerse yourself in the vocabulary. You develop the critical mass of people who have that philosophy, who get that it has to be collective and collaborative.

John stated that the ongoing application of inclusive concepts and an inclusive vocabulary by the whole-school initiative was crucial to more staff members becoming involved. Collaborative planning sessions allowed staff members to share information, learn from one another and guide the development of the initiative. This group of staff members could then share their knowledge, expertise and enthusiasm with others in the school.

While I was principal of a school located in an economically disadvantaged area, my staff members and I created a school-wide focus on empowering and supporting female student leadership and the development of self-esteem. The secondary school graduation rates for our female students were alarmingly low and, as a staff, we were determined to provide these students with more options. All members in the school community participated in a student-led and created activity. Our girls' leadership group – composed of fifteen to twenty senior-grade students – came up with the idea of supporting the local women's shelter. The group devised a school-wide plan and led a school-wide fundraiser to collect money, food, and clothing.

Nigel discussed how his school focused on African heritage throughout the year, instead of only during February, the one month typically devoted to Black history. That way, staff members and students had many opportunities to lead learning and connect with the community. He explained further,

> We made it more of a curriculum focus. Materials were provided for every teacher, [and we had] discussions and staff meetings about what we were going to do as a group. What kind of whole school things were we going to do? What kind of whole school events? We had a…really interesting assembly that was created by grade eight students and the librarian around influential and famous African-Canadians. We had daily announcements. We had a developing bulletin board. We had a "Heritage Night," an African heritage night with all kinds of events that were part of that.

This whole-school activity was imbedded in the curriculum design and expanded from there. There were materials for all staff members, plus opportunities for them to discuss their ideas. Students became involved as leaders as they discussed famous black Canadians, and events allowed parents and other community members to come to the school, so that the initiative included all stakeholders.

Todd stated that his school fundraised to support two or three charities each year. As the principal of a school located in a wealthy neighbourhood, he understood the importance of students learning that many people did not have the same material wealth as they did. Often the student council members chose the charities; they worked together with staff members to organize the events. He explained,

For instance, there might be a charity at a church down in the south part of our area that needs, say, Christmas baskets or Christmas boxes. Then [...] the classrooms likely will challenge each other to come up with as many boxes as they can. And there's just a huge outpouring of generosity when the kids do that. So that's tremendous work for the thing and it's through – I think through that charity work, I think – that the kids recognize the importance of charity and recognize that there are others that are far less fortunate and far less able than our community is.

Karen discussed how the teachers on her staff wanted to teach students to be more sensitive to the needs and lives of others. The solution Karen thought up was a whole-school initiative to sponsor a village in Sierra Leone. She explained,

We thought if we just took it out of the context first, to help them see the issues and feel some passion and compassion and some sense of doing things for others out there, that maybe we could bring it closer. And get the students, the parents, community, businesses, and, yeah, within a year they raised enough to build a school. And the second year they built a well and we bought, you know, goats and pigs and whatnot for the village. So [...] they learned a lot about this particular village in Sierra Leone, too. So it opened up their world a bit.

Karen explained that this whole-school activity brought the school community together and also provided an excellent segue to examining homelessness in their local community. Whereas there had previously been a stark divide between French and regular-stream students in her school, this project required both sets of students to work together on a common goal. Students from both groups became much more aware of the world around them. At the same time, they recognized that the boundaries between them were easier to overcome.

John told me how his school community created something called the "diversity mural project." He explained that the project involved principal, staff, parental volunteers, [and] community partners. We have the immigrant culture and arts association involved in that project. Every student in the school – every junior student in the school – participated in the whole project. And if you were to look at it, we are very proud of it. There is every background, culture, language, symbol, totem that was important to students at that point in time in these murals.

This whole-school activity not only provided an opportunity for people to work together, it also allowed them to communicate about their cultures and backgrounds. The activity allowed every student to contribute in a meaningful way since it showcased the different cultures and histories in the school population.

Debra's school was located in a very poor area. She used twice-yearly "fun fairs" to bring the community together. Debra knew that these fun fairs would not make money, but they would provide an opportunity for the community to meet. She explained,

Our parents don't have the funds. They wouldn't come because they know they can't afford it for their kids. So the only thing that costs them is the food, and the food is done by the businesses, the local businesses, like the local fish-and-chips store [...] And I said, the only condition is that you [keep the] prices [low] enough so our parents can afford it. So they [the businesses] are not going broke, but they are just making enough money to make a little bit of profit.

Debra understood that the purpose of the fun fairs was not to make money but to unite people. The parents in the community knew that she designed the fun fairs with that goal in mind.

Peter described how his school staff worked together to organize a snack-and-food program. Through discussions with staff and students, he realized that many students were coming to school hungry each day. Nineteen of twenty staff members participated in the school initiative and solicited volunteers from the local parish to cook and supervise. At first, staff members believed the initiative was "another duty," but they soon saw a major benefit of having such a program: it improved student behaviour throughout the day. Peter elaborated that the breakfast program had

> been eye-opening for everybody. They not only see how hungry [students] are, but they've also seen the kind of food that the people in the socioeconomic conditions that we serve eat, which is not typically what the teachers would see eaten in their own homes.

Staff members learned more about their students' lives through the initiative, and it also connected staff members and students in a very positive activity outside of the classroom.

Staff members, specifically teachers, are key to students being included in the school. By working with staff members, you have already begun taking steps to make your students feel included. In the next chapter, I'll outline some specific strategies that will further support the inclusion of students.

Growing Inclusion with Students

HOW DO WE SUPPORT OUR STUDENTS perceiving themselves to be "of" the school, rather than just in it? Some effective strategies revolve around leadership in the school; others deal with instruction and with school-wide initiatives such as anti-bullying and other safe-school policies and practices. Common to all effective strategies is that each student is viewed as a unique individual with distinct talents, experiences, and history. This means that opportunities within the school must be tailored specifically to your students. You can do this in two main ways: through encouraging student voice and leadership and through instituting instruction and programming that supports the inclusion of all students.

Student Voice and Leadership

Do you provide ongoing opportunities for students to share their beliefs about all aspects of your school? Do they also have opportunities to lead or to share leadership with other school participants? Ensuring that students have a voice and the power to influence and shape the school is paramount to including them.

Student input and leadership are often overlooked when school improvement or similar-minded reforms are tabled. And there will always be some educators who raise concerns that chaos will result if students are given more power. Encourage student voice and power anyway. My experience has taught me that the more power students have, the better the school operates in all ways.

i) Older students as leaders. Some of the principals I spoke to had sought out leadership opportunities for older students within their schools. These opportunities were not always part of the school's formal structure, and they took place in a variety of ways. Nigel stated that there were many difficulties with helping the special education students in his school feel included. He explained,

> We had kids in our special ed. classes who were having terrible social problems at recess. So we found ways to [include them]. We had a thing called "the Super-Heroes Club" where we had social skills groups for those kids.

Nigel explained that he had had grade eight students take leadership roles to support the special education students. The older students worked together to slowly integrate the special education students into the school-yard. It was a case of students helping students. And the grade eight students, by being in leadership roles, became more cognizant of the special education students' need for support.

John highlighted how student leaders had worked together with the school secretary to support ESL students. The secretary acted as the staff lead on this initiative. The student leaders acted as ESL tutors, working directly with students who needed extra support. The tutors not only supported other students, but learned about the ESL students' school experiences.

Kristin chose her school's leadership team from students in grades four, five and six, because her school did not have grades seven or eight. These students were involved in the school in a variety of ways. As she explained,

> the purpose is to give kids the chance to lead an assembly, to do the morning announcements, to see themselves taking charge of various things around the school. So they help out with the primary play-day. When we do our jump program in the spring, they are out there helping with that.

The students at Kristin's school worked together as a leadership team while taking guidance from certain staff members. As well, by having students in grades four through six on the team, there was a complement of experienced and new members each year.

Dave cited the use at his school of a conflict resolution program that involved students in important leadership positions. He explained,

> We didn't take the kids that were the most conflict-resolution-ready to become the peacemakers. But [we] really tried to make it a mixed group so that there were some of those kids. But there were also kids for whom the training would provide a new way for them to begin thinking about things, and that other kids would all of a sudden see them as peacemakers, as opposed to what they normally saw them as.

It is significant that the students chosen were not always the ones who were the most skilled at resolving disputes. Leadership opportunities in Dave's school were not offered only to students who already met the requirements for the position. Some students who were chosen as peacemakers were not yet ready for the position, but staff members believed the leadership program would provide them with excellent training. This gave all students a chance to demonstrate that they could contribute something positive to the school community.

Nina described how grade six, seven, and eight students were involved in numerous leadership activities around her school. These students organized school dances, spirit days, and fundraising activities. By having students involved in leadership activities throughout the year, there was a greater likelihood of student leadership becoming part of the daily fabric of the school.

Matt was principal of two different schools within one building: an alternative middle school and a multicultural junior school. When he first arrived, there were no leadership activities for students and very little interaction between the two schools. Matt elaborated,

> When I first got there, there was nothing. Now there is a leadership program for the grade eights – because it's a middle school – and they work once a week in a classroom in the junior school. [There's] kind of a buddy system with some of the other kids, and they have run play-date again as the leadership.

This new structure provided leadership experiences for older students while at the same time connecting the two schools.

As Matt's experience shows, students in the senior grades often enjoy working with primary students, and vice-versa. Some teachers use weekly reading buddies or school-spirit day activities to allow classes at different levels to get together.

ii) Using a student council. Student councils provide students with leadership opportunities and give them a voice to discuss student needs. The student council in many schools is a formal structure that involves democratic elections and specific roles for student leaders. Since the first couple of weeks in September are so busy, I aim to have the student council at my school formed by the end of that month. Prior to that, teachers can talk to students about the role of the student council in the school, the election process and the expectations of the students who are elected (that they be good listeners, act as role models, be collaborative with others, etcetera). Student councils provide most students' first experience with the democratic process, and they learn very quickly how important their voices are considered to be in the school. Throughout the year, I seek advice and input from student council members on a variety of topics. Student input makes my decisions or solutions more effective and reinforces the critical point that students are valued and capable members of the school community.

Todd used student representatives from each classroom to form the school government, which raised money for charities and developed ideas for spirit days. The students led and organized these activities, and through them gained an understanding of the lives of people who were struggling financially. Todd stressed how important he felt it was for his students to understand how privileged their own lives were.

John indicated that student council members were vital in providing students with a voice in his school. He set a goal for the student council members: to raise money for the school's "Kenyan Adopt a Village" initiative. Giving them a common goal was one method of bringing the student council membership together. John also stated that it was important to work directly with individual student council members, so that they learned how to define their opinions and how to conduct themselves during meetings.

Dave scheduled regular meetings for grade eight students that were led either by staff or by student council members. The student council members

> would bring up the issues that they wanted to talk about that were important to them, things they thought should change. Sometimes, they would come up with whatever the idea was, and then they would come and meet with me. We would discuss what was going to happen, how it would be implemented. [I was always] very positive in terms of letting them understand how change can happen. And that it doesn't always have to be [top-down], that [the] student voice is important in a school.

The dialogue at Dave's school was two-way between students and staff members. These discussions allowed students to offer ideas about how to improve the school and taught them how the process of making change operated.

Tony outlined the need to provide ongoing training for student council members so that they could be more effective. He explained,

> You want kids involved, you want them to have a say, but oftentimes, they're not sophisticated enough to have the proper say. "Oh yeah, we want dances." Okay, you want dances. We started a student council. And first, we started it with younger kids. So we had grade five to grade eight kids involved in our student council. We provided those kids with leadership training, as well.

Students at Tony's school had ideas, but they needed to develop their skills at organizing and implementing these initiatives. By having students from a variety of different grades on the student council, he ensured that younger students would be able to apply the leadership training they received in the years to come.

Peter included the student council members on certain committees in his school. He elaborated,

We would often invite the student council representative to sit on some committees that were appropriate for them to do so. So we would often try to develop inclusion between the staff and students. There were three committees where we included parents and students [...] to develop inclusion amongst all three.

Peter gave the example of a healthy-food committee that involved parents, staff members, and student council members. The student council members were included in the decision-making and the discussion about how to promote healthy eating. Having students participate on school-wide committees is an important way of ensuring that their voices will be heard.

iii) Providing other leadership experiences for students. Some principals I spoke to gave examples of less formal types of student leadership than those offered on student councils. These experiences could be regular occurrences in the school or short-term initiatives or programs. Brent ensured that all of his senior students were involved in leadership experiences and training. For example, he mentioned that grade seven students took leadership roles in health and anti-bullying initiatives. As he explained,

> I've never been in favor of student councils, simply because they do become cliquish and elitist. You get a few popular kids [who] get voted in all the time, and they tend not to be as productive [in terms of] simply sharing leadership as broadly as possible amongst the school. And so what we do, for example, is [that] all of our grade eights participate in leadership opportunities throughout the school. [...] All of our grade eight and seven students in the schools I've been in are assigned, as part of their community service for their confirmation preparation, to be readers for the PA announcements and the "O Canada" and all the different elements that go on in the school. So we try to give our kids as much profile as possible.

One of Brent's goals was to share out the leadership experiences among his students so that no one student was singled out or favored. He wanted to be more inclusive with leadership training, so that all students would have these experiences.

Craig told me that his school's Global Awareness Club provided leadership and learning experiences for students. He explained,

> The Global Awareness [Club] will tell you about the latest holiday in some culture… it's more intense than a club; it's close to the school student council. So that's the perk, they get to do that. They do the work or create the posters. They know how to have some guest speakers in. They have special suppers. They'll stay after school and do different kinds of food that are not their own culture and they'll cook it all up and celebrate.

The club was open to any student in the school, and the leadership experiences were connected to students developing an understanding of the world.

Sports teams, intramurals and clubs within your school dramatically support inclusion. These experiences allow students from different grades and classes to gather for a shared interest. The activities are usually led by staff members who volunteer to help, and your dedication to supporting staff holistically will set the table for clubs and activities.

Instruction and Programming

Students' learning needs must also be addressed through effective programming and teaching. Students who fall behind academically lose interest in learning and feel like outsiders in their own classrooms. Given the diversity of the learning needs, the solutions you devise for your school must also be multi-faceted.

i) **Collaboration and team teaching.** Encouraging teachers to work together and share pedagogical insights and expertise will help your school meet the academic needs of your students. Principals can support collaboration among staff members by timetabling common prep times, and also by ensuring that there are ongoing collaborative activities during staff meetings, on professional development days, and as part of the school-improvement plan. As well, principals can shift teaching assignments to ensure that grade or division teams are better suited to work together. The end result is that students' experiences at school are the responsibility of all staff members, not simply of the classroom teachers.

ii) Special education support in the general classroom. Instead of withdrawing special education students from the general classrooms, special education teachers can visit them there. Consistent with the emphasis on team teaching and collaboration, special education teachers and classroom teachers can work together to develop appropriate programs and deliver these to students. The immediate benefits of team teaching include: a) the sharing of pedagogical and planning knowledge to support the learning of all students in the class; b) the implementation of individualized education plans for special education students; c) the inclusion of special education students, who no longer feel centred out because instruction is delivered in the class; and d) opportunities for more peer-support mechanisms in the classroom.

iii) Differentiated instruction. In every class there is a diversity of student learning needs. There will be students who have been identified as learning disabled or requiring extra support. Some students will still be learning English, while others would benefit from accelerated learning. Differentiated instruction is a vital classroom strategy for including all students. Using a lesson in which all students share the same content, and are made to follow the same process toward the same end product, will exclude students. Instead, teachers must identify each student's interests, reading and learning profile (Tomlinson and Allan 2000, 3).

iv) Comprehensive literacy programming in all classrooms. Effective programming and instruction include students in their classroom. It is not enough to work on all other areas of growing inclusion if classroom programming and instruction are sub-standard and not tailored to the individual student.

v) Culturally relevant teaching. Culturally relevant teaching (CRT) practices will help teachers to meet the learning needs of the diverse student population. The goal of this pedagogy is to increase academic achievement (Howard 2003, 196), but I would argue further that CRT also enhances students' self-esteem. In CRT, teachers incorporate the various cultures of their students into curriculum planning and delivery (Milner 2011, 69). Students then see themselves reflected both in the curriculum and the pedagogy. As Durden (2008) asserts,

> as learners, whenever we attempt to make sense of our world, we construct an understanding of the event by using our prior knowledge, past experiences, and cultural references as tools (410).

The key component here is to establish a connection between the students' school experiences and their lived reality. In CRT, for example, literacy activities are aligned to a student's culture, as opposed to standardized model examples (411). During the past two years in my school, Aboriginal students have been offered the choice of Mohawk language instruction instead of instruction in the other second language, French. Three months into the first year, both staff and students were amazed at the gains these students had made in their fluency. When I asked one student why he had learned more Mohawk in three months than he had learned French in three years, he responded, "Because the language is about who I am." His answer hit the mark: the curriculum and pedagogy were connected with his culture. In CRT, students are also encouraged to question and challenge the information and knowledge systems of the larger society. Ladson-Billings (1992) argues that this approach serves,

> to empower students to the point where they will be able to examine critically educational content and process and ask what its role is in creating a truly democratic and multicultural society. It uses the students' culture to help them create meaning and understand the world. Thus, not only academic success, but also social and cultural success is emphasized (in Milner 2010, 68).

When CRT is employed, students are not merely accepting information, they are learning to analyze it critically, with direct reference to the dominant culture. As they develop this critical consciousness, they start to understand how the power structures in society marginalize certain groups.

vi) Assessment using both quantitative and qualitative data. A holistic approach to education requires that all facets of a student's development – social, physical, emotional, and intellectual – be considered when measuring success. For example, a student who is making academic progress but having difficulty emotionally warrants extra support and attention from school staff.

vii) Ongoing student-success meetings. Formally organized student-success meetings at least once a month will allow staff members to share concerns and information on how all students are doing. Some schools organize these by specific grades or divisions. These student-success meetings do not preclude, of course, regular staff meetings, at which staff may share concerns of a more immediate nature. Some key aspects include: i) that all staff understand the holistic focus on student success; ii) that meetings involve a variety of staff members who bring different levels of expertise and/or experience; iii) that communication with the student's parent or guardian is ongoing; iv) that the individual student's voice is included, as is appropriate for his or her age; v) that an action plan covering next steps, participant responsibilities and timelines, is produced at every meeting.

The common thread running through all of these strategies for growing inclusion with students is knowing who your students are and what your school can do to support them holistically. In nearly all cases, offering this kind of support entails the school changing, not the student. Students will tell us about their school experiences and their hopes if we are there to listen. Just as the different forms of assessment provide us with solid data on student learning, listening to understand gives us extremely valuable information on our students' experiences in school. The qualitative and quantitative information you gather will be your guide to constructing appropriate programs and supports.

Students and teachers working together for a common purpose is further strengthened when parents are part of the team. In the next chapter, I'll focus on that third important group, outlining some strategies for growing inclusion with parents.

Growing Inclusion
with Parents

A PLETHORA OF RESEARCH DEMONSTRATES the relationship between the involvement of parents/guardians in a child's education and that child's academic achievement. We all know this. The tougher question, however, is how to encourage more parents'/guardians' involvement. All of the issues that affect our students – racism, classism, homophobia, prior negative experiences with schools, etcetera – also affect their parents/guardians. Views that marginalize students have marginalized their parents/guardians as well. The challenges of including all parents/guardians can be more daunting since many do not belong to the dominant culture, and so have experienced lifetimes of marginalization, oppression and exclusion. For these reasons, we cannot evaluate a parent's commitment to the school or determine how he or she values education based on how many times the agendas we send home are signed, how many phone calls are returned, how often the parent/guardian attends school meetings, events, or interviews.

We have all heard the statements: "The parents in this community don't care about school," or "The parents in this school don't care about their kids." These observations focus on people through a deficit lens. I get my back up very quickly when I hear this type of statement. As a beginning teacher, I remember telling my church's minister one day that many of my students' parents did not care about education. The minister was a calm and level-headed individual, and he stopped me quickly. "You are there not to judge anyone but to teach and serve your student," he told me. Twenty years later, his words still resonate with me. We simply cannot define the participation or commitment of parents/guardians using a dominant-culture lens. What do we know about their lives and their own experiences in school as students? Are they working three jobs to make ends meet? Do illnesses or language limit their ability to communicate and participate? Have their experiences with their children's schools to date been positive or negative?

Newsletters, mass emails, and school community events are all avenues for communicating the school foci to parents, but it is one-to-one communication that will build trust. With trust in place, you have the opportunity to grow inclusion. Parents must not only be genuinely included in the school; they must also understand how their children are included, that we have high expectations for their holistic progress, and that we care.

Making "Parents as Partners" a school-wide priority.

"Parents as Partners" is a simple phrase, but a critical one for school participants. The importance of including parents should be written into your school's improvement or continued-growth plan. What steps are the school taking to make "parents as partners" a reality? What do these expectations look like at the classroom level? As noted earlier, communicating your views on inclusion to your staff is critical, and parents should be included in this larger vision from the outset. There is no need to wait six months for a school committee to determine that parents are important members of the school community and should be involved.

The principals I spoke to identified different strategies for promoting inclusion with their students' parents/guardians. These strategies included: 1) using parents as links to other parents; 2) working collaboratively with school council members; 3) communicating with parents in a variety of ways; 4) educating parents about inclusion; 5) connecting parents with community organizations; and 6) being available to listen.

i) Using parents as links to other parents. Several principals identified certain parents they could rely on to communicate with other parents about the school. Word-of-mouth works quickly, covering all aspects of the school; many of these conversations take place on the school grounds prior to entry in the morning, while parents and children are waiting. The interactions you and your staff have with parents have a "ripple effect" that can either encourage or discourage participation.

Nigel, a principal of a multicultural school in a large urban area, described how he received help in connecting with the school's Chinese parents.

> I have some conduits to the Chinese community, for instance. So I have some people I talk to who I believe are somewhat representative, who will bring things to me, [who] I've encouraged to do that.

As one example, Nigel learned through these parents that many parents in the Chinese community wanted to come into the school at lunch to spend time with their sons and daughters. Based on this information, he gave parents permission to eat lunch with their children at school. This became a regular practice and served as a starting point for listening to Chinese parents' other needs.

John described how he spent time with a parent of Turkish descent in his school. Over a few months, he built up trust with this parent, and eventually the parent confided in him. She was seeking help for another parent in the community, was able to get it when she told her friend that the principal was someone who could be trusted.

Dave worked in a school with many Vietnamese students and he wanted their parents to come into the school more often. Through a translator, he was able to communicate with those parents to learn more about their lives. This information was then passed on to staff members. He stated,

> We would hire somebody who spoke Vietnamese to actually phone parents and explain to them and try to get them to come in. If you phoned […] a few would come. But generally speaking, we found out that […] the reason they don't come is because they work three jobs and they really can't come.

The translator provided the Vietnamese parents at the school with a voice and a way to communicate with school staff. Staff members, for their part, gained valuable information about the lives of these parents and developed other strategies to more effectively include them in the school.

Tony worked in a school in which the majority of the population was made up of students of colour. He wanted to include more of their parents in the school, and he sought the help of one parent in particular to achieve this. Tony elaborated,

> I had one of the non-white parents... I asked her if she would gather a number of non-white parents who might be willing to come in and chat anytime. So they decided Saturday. So we met over three or four Saturdays just to chat [....] I wanted to get to know them, and I wanted to understand what their concerns were, and I wanted to also try to get an idea of how to get them into school.

The first parent served as the starting point for communication between Tony and a group of other parents. Their meetings took place off school property, on the weekend. By attending these meetings, Tony demonstrated to the parents that he valued their input and wanted them involved with the school. He also worked collaboratively with the grandparent of one of his students to devise strategies to help foster the relationship between the school and parents. Tony was open to trying new ideas and to learning from this grandparent's experiences to support inclusion.

Susan stated that in her school she worked with several parents who acted as liaisons with the larger community. These parents spoke the various languages of the community, and they supported the communication between school and parents. To ensure inclusion, it was critical that communication about school issues and events be carried out in several languages, not simply English.

Matt also worked with parents in his community to enhance positive communication between home and school. He elaborated:

There are other key parents whom I recognize as being sympathetic to the goals of the school, or understanding the goals of the school, and, hopefully, the good intentions of the school and the staff. And it's a word-of-mouth advertising kind of campaign, so that there is a balance in the discussion that we know is happening out in the neighbourhood, the proverbial parking-lot discussions. You know it's going on out there, and so you want to encourage and supply good information to the people who are pro-school.

These liaison parents helped Matt to learn about what was happening in parents' and students' lives. Just as importantly, they advocated for the school to other parents and community members.

ii) Working collaboratively with school council or P.T.A. members. Many principals told me that they worked with the school council members to promote the inclusion of parents in the school. In some school systems, these associations are known as Parent-Teacher Associations (PTA). Formal structures like school councils or PTAs provide the framework for parents to have a voice in how the school operates.

Todd explained that the two co-chairs of his school council had been outstanding, providing "excellent leadership and direction for the parents." He worked well with these co-chairs on building inclusion in his school.

Karen also worked with school council members to get more parents involved. She had noticed, over the years, that school council members did not come from all the different social classes of the school. For that reason, she explained,

I talked to the school council chair about that in both of those schools when I first arrived. And then we talked to the [...] incoming members, the members of school council that were already there, and everyone did agree that it would be a good idea to make some phone calls and see if we could get more diverse representation.

Even with their combined efforts, it was a challenge to make the council more diverse, but Karen cited the skill of the council chair as key to the initiative's success.

> The chair was excellent. I would say she was a very inclusive person herself [...] She was very deliberate in making sure that she solicited voices from people around the table, you know, rather than just waiting for people to speak up. It's tough. It's tough for people who aren't used to feeling as though they're in positions of influence.

The school council chair shared Karen's commitment to inclusion and took specific steps to ensure participation by all members of the school council.

Kristin had learned, over the years, that the school council members did not always know what the greater school community wanted or needed. Some council members, for instance, wondered why there were parenting workshops taking place in the school. From feedback like this, Karen understood that the council's ideas were not representative of the many different views in the parents' community. The parent workshops in her school, she told me, were "what attracts the multicultural group." Kristin knew from the council's response that she would need to guide the selection of events aimed to connect with the school community. The school council members needed her help both to create opportunities that would attract a more diverse group of parents and to understand the importance of these inclusive gestures.

In Dave's school, there were usually fifty people at each school council meeting. Three co-chairs worked on the meeting agendas, so they would represent the many different views in the community. Dave worked with co-chairs at the outset to help them decide on the issues and ideas they wanted to look at during the year, as well as topics for specific meetings. By taking extra time to meet with the three of them privately, Dave helped facilitate the success of these meetings.

Debra adjusted the scheduling of her school council meetings so that more parents could attend. As she explained,

> So I have a council meeting Thursday evening, followed
> by a Friday daytime council meeting, just to accommodate
> the different schedules for the parents. So that way we have
> [more] parents involved.

Having the two meeting times demonstrated to parents that the school council was an important component of the school, and that the school was attempting to support the parents' needs. While this two-meeting approach required Debra to devote extra time to the meetings, she was able to meet with different groups of parents on the same issues. She also provided daycare to help families during these meeting times.

Tony identified the importance of the school council chairs, whom he said were very interested in "moving the school forward and were very supportive" of his efforts to promote an inclusive environment. One of these chairs would come to school council meetings held on Saturdays for parents of all backgrounds who felt isolated, so that she could learn more about their needs. Tony said that this school council chair was important because she brought a "different view" to the discussion table; the Saturday meetings provided different groups of parents with opportunities to share their viewpoints and ideas concerning the school. One of the key elements here is that this school council chair saw the need to have more representation on the school council; the status quo was not adequate.

iii) Communicating with parents using a variety of methods. Ongoing communication is key to building bridges with parents, and utilizing a variety of ways to deliver information and to hear about parent concerns and ideas greatly supports an inclusive school. Monthly newsletters sent home are simply not enough. Information sent out via a mass email, now a common practice in schools, can be problematic for families who do not have regular access to computers or the Internet. It is important to find different ways to get out the information, even to over-communicate what is happening at the school and how the students are doing. The critical questions for determining successful communication are:

a) *Do our parents know what the school's goals and foci are?*

b) *Do our parents hear on a regular basis how their children are doing in school, in a holistic sense?*

c) *Do our parents have ongoing opportunities to communicate with school staff members?*

There are, of course, challenges that arise when trying to ensure that communication is ongoing and frequent. Each of these challenges, however – be it time, staff-member commitment to communication, parents' work schedules, or language – can and must be overcome.

Nigel, as a principal of a multicultural school in which many different languages were spoken, explained that he placed a lot of emphasis on providing support to parents whose first language was not English.

> One of the pieces is the language piece to develop an inclusion with parents [...] That's always a difficulty. Being a Toronto school, we have a great deal of diversity. But we have interpreters. We have letters going home in other languages.

Karen highlighted two methods she used to communicate with parents. First, she made certain that the staff were able to schedule interviews during the school day. As she explained,

> In one particular school, there was quite a large faction of the local community that did a fair bit of shift work. And so, you know, interviews from four to seven is when they're at work. And before school in the morning is difficult, because they have to sleep sometimes. So, my expectation always was that you [the teacher] would find a time, a mutual time, when it could work.

If a parent wanted to schedule an interview during school hours, then Karen would facilitate that happening. Second, Karen used private conversations with parents in a variety of locales to ensure they felt included in the school. She cited one example of a parent who did not feel comfortable being in the school building, yet needed to speak to her about his two daughters. Both of them had special education concerns, and he was very defensive about this situation. As Karen remembered,

> the kind of conversation I could have with him leaning against his car, you know, across the street from the school, was vastly different [than in the school]. That was his comfort zone. There were often lots of things I needed to speak with him about. And there's a whole other story there about things having been put in motion to have these two girls shipped off to a classroom in another school, and he didn't want that to happen.

By meeting this father across the street, Karen provided a more comfortable venue for him to discuss his two daughters. She also met parents at the local Tim Horton's restaurant to discuss an issue or concern. She understood that discussion about school did not always have to take place on school property, and that not all parents wanted to meet there.

Kristin made certain that in every newsletter from her school, and at every presentation for a trip or activity, she told people they could contact her about financial issues. She knew there were families in her school who were struggling financially, and they usually contacted her by telephone. When Kristin responded to these phone calls, she was always sensitive in her use of language.

> I say the same thing to everybody: "Is there an amount that you are able to pay?" And [I] let them identify what that amount is. [In] one case it was zero, and in another case it was all but twenty-five dollars. And I don't make the assumption that they don't want to contribute something. I ask them directly, "Is there an amount that you feel you can handle?" And if they say "No," then that is fine and I will handle the bill. If they say, "I can handle ten dollars," then I say, "Okay, we will be handling the other $135.00 and just send in the ten dollars."

Kristin wanted to ensure that all children had the financial means to participate in trips or activities without compromising their parents' pride. She also conveyed the message about possible school support as many times throughout the year as possible. This is an important point; sometimes the same message needs to be given many times in order for others to receive it. Kristin also provided parents with an opportunity to share in the paying of the field trips or activities; each case was different, but all parents were included in the final decision.

Similarly, Allan cited the importance of daily discussions with parents. He remembered that, years earlier, he had started as principal of a school in January and wanted to bring in school uniforms. The initial response from parents was only 69% in favour. Allan then began private conversations with parents. As he explained,

> I worked those parents then. I worked them, I talked to them, I talked about the value. I put up a bulletin board, a display cabinet myself, on the benefits of school uniforms. Parents who challenged the notion of school uniforms – you know what? I did not cuss them out. I said, "I want to learn from you. Come on, and let's have a chat. Teach me what you know. Tell me what you think is wrong with school uniforms." And we talked, and we talked, and we talked.

Through many, many one-to-one conversations, Allan was able to communicate with a large number of parents. The process took place over months, and it was time-intensive. He reported that the number of parents in favour of uniforms by the end was 87%; this increase was largely due to his commitment to those individual discussions. They helped him to understand parents' concerns and let parents learn about his reasoning.

Debra made sure that her school always communicated with parents in more than one language. As she explained,

> When I send my newsletters out, there is always one section in my newsletter written by four different parents. And all it says, in their own [respective] language[s], is "to get this translated." So for Chinese it would say: "to get this translated in Chinese" – and it's written in Chinese – "call" – and it's a parent volunteer. And these parent volunteers are very active in our school as far as council [goes], as far as coming

in and talking to us about issues or concerns or organizing big events. So we have four parents who do that.

These four parents helped connect the school and parents by translating, but also by representing the different groups in the school. Having the newsletters include four other languages in addition to English was a visual and written reminder to parents in the community that the school wanted to hear from them, and that communication between home and school is important. Even if the school staff cannot speak to all of these parents in their mother tongues, these parents were still included in the school community.

Anna had great difficulty getting parents to attend school council meetings. She had discovered, however, that whenever the school had a movie night, the attendance was excellent. Anna came up with an idea.

> I'm thinking, you know how they have little commercials before the movie? I'm thinking, okay, if we have another movie night, we'll talk about literacy or talk about home reading and why it's important prior to [...] [the] show. It's a captive audience! [I thought,] you know what? I'm going to try that. I'm going to try putting something in and then showing the movie.

Anna's idea was a success, with more parents learning more about their children's school lives.

Susan used the monthly school council meetings to communicate with parents, but she also held monthly "meet and greets." In these "meet and greets," parents, the principal and the vice-principal, and other staff members sat in a circle and discussed issues. Each person in the circle had an opportunity to talk about anything he or she wanted to. As Susan remembered,

> At the first meet and greet, I had only been here a few weeks, and one of the parents said – it was around the time that they were looking at same-sex marriages – and so one of the parents said out loud in front of everybody, "We really don't believe in same-sex marriages or anything even

slightly like same-sex." So I laughed, and I said to her, "Oh, that's good that we're starting off with a very hard point." And I said to her that – she had asked me for support for their position – and I said to her that there was no way that I was going to be able to support her position, because it was against human rights and it was against the board's equity document.

These monthly gatherings gave parents the opportunity to meet with school staff members in a very inclusive setting. There were no assigned seats, and there was an informal and welcoming nature to the meetings. Each person present had ample opportunity to discuss any issue.

When Peter wanted to find out about parents' and students' concerns, he sent out letters, used the phone, and met with parents on the playground to gather information. He knew that personal communication with individual parents would be the most effective way to get the feedback he needed. Because he did not rely on any single method of communication, he was able to gather a wealth of information.

iv) Educating parents about inclusion. Some of the principals I spoke to indicated that educating parents about inclusion was an effective strategy. Parents, like staff members, needed to learn about inclusion in order to understand and value it. Karen knew that her school council members were not representative of the cultural and socioeconomic diversity in the school. She talked with them about getting more members from the various groups. As she explained,

> It wasn't a matter of them [school council members] being deliberately exclusionary. It was, "Oh, I guess you're right. I hadn't really thought about it that way." I mean, we're not talking about evildoers who are trying to keep people outside the door. But sometimes you just have to have someone help you notice things, because you just get used to things being as they are.

By having that discussion with the school council members, Karen helped them understand that the current school council membership was not representative of all the groups in the school. She made it clear that keeping things the same was not an option. Moreover, Karen believed that once parents were made aware of injustices, they would be willing to help remedy them. This motivated her to point out inequities wherever she saw them, always ensuring that she suggested solutions.

Kristin noticed that her school council members did not seem aware of the cultural and economic diversity in her school. She lamented,

> They [school council members] are not aware, I don't think, about [the fact] that it is all one economic group [on council], [and] that they are all white. I don't think that really occurs to them. I don't think they see it as a problem.

For this reason, Kristin worked hard first to develop the awareness of her school council members concerning the varying interests and groups in the school, and then to ensure that these diverse groups were genuinely represented on school council. Her challenge was to get the established council to understand how others were being excluded.

Debra also worked on increasing parents' awareness of the plight of some students in her school. She elaborated,

> Even our parents, they don't really get what life is for some of their friends [or] their children's friends. They really don't. So when I sit down, I have a heart-to-heart discussion with them. You know, when I say, "I am sorry I didn't get back to you yesterday. I am getting back to you today because I was dealing with this child who has no food." They go, "Well, what do you mean they have no food? Everyone has food." I said, "No. Everyone doesn't have food." And so [this parent] gets this understanding of when children are stealing lunches, it's not because they are bad kids. They have no other way of getting the food. So that's an eye-opening experience for everybody.

v) Connecting parents with community organizations. Several principals said that they used community organizations to support inclusion in their elementary schools. Individuals from these organizations worked with staff members or on their own in the school to promote the inclusion of parents. John mentioned that his community settlement worker, Gita, was vital in helping him connect the parents with the school. As he explained,

> I could take advantage of her skills and her prominence on the playground to begin to establish relationships, and that worked. Over time, the parents would work through Gita to get to me. And then it became almost – I just described something linear; it became something very, very circular, so lots of success there.

Although Gita was not a board employee, parents saw her as part of the school. Gita connected with parents and then worked to support their communication and interaction with school staff members.

Dave gave three examples of how he used community agencies to help him include students, parents, and community members in the school. His school was located in one of the poorest areas of the city and was significantly affected by government cuts. As he explained,

> Everybody in that community was affected by losing about a fifth of their income, which was already unmanageable to begin with. So the school, at that time, working with community agencies, worked with residents and organized an evening for them at the community centre where parents just were able to come and talk about what these cuts meant to them, and just to have a voice around what was happening.

These community meetings took place in the school, and they provided parents with an opportunity to meet and work directly with the various agencies. As Dave pointed out, these meetings also made staff members and parents aware that they had common interests, and that they could work together. Moreover, by bringing the community agencies together in one central location, Dave made it easier for parents to meet one another and to learn about supports.

As his second example, Dave explained that he had invited Somali community workers to come to the school and speak with staff about the civil war in Somalia and about Somali culture. Through those conversations, staff members learned more about the lives and experiences of their students and how better to support them in school.

Third, Dave met with various agencies to figure out how to help his students attend after-school programs in the community. He started these initiatives in 2000, a year he called the "year of the gun" in his city. Parents were truly afraid for their children to be outside after school hours. Community programs were suffering a significant lack of after-school participation as a result. As Dave explained,

> We started this thing called "Safe Walk Home." We applied for funding and got it, outside funding. The youth, high school youth, in the community were trained to be walkers, so they went to these training classes about what it meant to be a walker, how to do it. Then the kids, the little kids in the elementary schools, [their] parents would sign them up and it was like a real signing-up thing. And each walker would come to a school and pick up kids and then walk them to the after-school program, and then pick them up at the end of their after-school program and walk them [home]. And,[…] somebody had to sign for them when they got home.

This solution involved school staff working directly with parents and community agencies. Together, they created a solution. Everyone gained from the solution.

Debra had a community worker who met weekly with parents in her school. All questions or concerns could be raised with this worker at the group meeting. Debra understood that having a forum of this kind, in which parents discussed issues, was important. As she explained,

> It's a drop in. And sometimes I am there. I said, "I need to be invited to this." I will not come in on a regular basis, because sometimes parents just need to meet. And if they want to complain about the school, they need to know the principal is not sitting there as they are complaining about the school. So I said, "By invitation, I will come in. I will drop in every once in a while, but by invitation."

Debra knew the importance of parents having a safe place to discuss and share their concerns about the school. She attended these meetings only when she was invited. In this way, she demonstrated her respect for the autonomy of the discussion group.

Susan described creating many opportunities and places within her school for parents to meet, and gave a few examples.

> We have a parenting centre for parents and young children. We also have on-site three portables that are used by the Somali Women-and-Children's Network. And they service not only Somali women, but [...] women from all different nationalities. They teach them English. There are five different levels, and there's been advocacy there, too, in terms of getting them another portable. There were many steps that had to happen to get them another portable that they could use on the school property. And they have daycare for the children while they are learning English. They also teach them employability skills, so they learn sewing and computer skills.

These community programs within the school provided parents with many valuable services to help them in their daily lives. One important part of these programs was the support for all family members within the school during school hours. Women could attend after they had dropped their children off at school or use the daycare service affiliated with the program.

Susan also explained that parts of her school were used as a community centre to offer parenting programs at night. She sought partnerships with three different community organizations to provide the funding for the programs that took place. As she outlined,

> The school is a hub of activity until around 9:30 at night. There are hundreds of people walking around all the time, and I often will work late. They often will come see me in the evenings. They'll poke on the glass, or whatever, they know I'm here so they come to visit me. So the school is always open, and it's always very, very active.[...] There's summer camps for Parks and Rec. So the school is always

a hub of community involvement and activity. It's a very busy place.

These community programs included the parents in Susan's school and connected them with her. The parents saw the school as the "centre" of the community. Susan devoted time to building these community connections with parents, sought funding and advocated for space. In these ways, parents and students felt that the school belonged to them.

Nina wanted to get the parents and the students in her school more involved in the community centre located next door. She worked collaboratively with a local police officer, and one of their goals was to engage the students after school in positive programs. But Nina also knew that many families could not afford to pay for these programs, so she sought ways to make them affordable. As she explained,

> My husband and I, being former phys. ed. teachers, came down and trained police officers on how to run a recreational program. So they [these police officers] volunteered for the programs, we trained them. A group of teachers ran arts and crafts at [the community centre] after school one day a week for an hour, and then a mother did a dance class. So there were three nights of the week and that was our start to bring[ing] kids out into the community, and community members out to the kids.

Nina went on to seek additional support from community organizations for these programs, because she could not continue volunteering three nights a week while working full-time as a principal. She included in these discussions the school superintendent, the superintendent of police, city councilors, and staff from the community centre. She also connected with people through a school-community hub committee that included parents, school, and community centre staff members. The committee met to discuss community issues and solutions. Nina told me that all of these initiatives were instrumental in connecting to and including parents in her school.

Many parents need support and guidance to learn about the resources in the community and how to access them. From my own experience as a principal, I know there are also times when parents will ask one of the school staff to go to an appointment with them and their children. Meeting this request, besides being the moral thing to do, supports both the family and the child in your school. Keep in mind that school is only one of the many institutions in our society that marginalize people. Parents often have had negative experiences with these institutions, and they need our support and input as educators.

vi) Being visible on the playground before and after school. Before and after school are excellent times for principals to dialogue with parents. These informal discussions, over time, go a long way toward making parents feel welcome and increasing their understanding of what the school's foci are. Remember, too, that it often takes repeated information interactions before many parents feel comfortable discussing issues of importance.

vii) Growing inclusion one parent at a time. There are many instances throughout the week where parents will seek your help or guidance on a variety of issues. The same holds true for staff members. How you and your staff interact with these parents is key, since each meeting or interaction is a building block for tomorrow.

viii) Continuing to learn about parents' lives and experiences. As outlined, lack of parent participation at school events or functions does not mean that parents are not interested in their child's education. Throughout the year, it is important to devote staff time to increasing your understanding of the obstacles and barriers parents may be facing. Without that, we can fall prey to deficit thinking.

At one of my previous schools, for example, parent turnout for "Meet the teacher night" was terribly low, and it had been that way for many years. From conversations with parents on the playground over the next few weeks, I learned that many parents found the time selected for their meetings too early in the day; many were just returning from work. The traditional time met the needs of the staff members, but not of the parents. The following year, we changed the time based on direct input from parents, and the turnout was substantially better.

ix) Being available to listen. When my younger son Matthew was five, he came to one of the school's evening concerts. Seeing the gymnasium full, with over five hundred people, he asked if I was the boss of all these people. When I said no, he asked what I did all day, then. He was disappointed to learn that I spent much of my day listening. The value of being available to listen to parents' concerns or ideas cannot be overestimated. The more we know about the lives, experiences, and histories of our students and their families, the better we'll be able to serve them.

There are numerous strategies or practices you and your school can use to grow inclusion. But, as we all know, the day we plan is rarely how the day goes. The role of principal is an incredibly demanding and stressful one, and growing inclusion cannot occur without others. There are allies within the school community who support growing inclusion, and there are also barriers that serve to constrict or limit any or all growth. In the next chapter I describe the barriers and allies to growing inclusion.

Overcoming Barriers and Cultivating Allies

AS PRINCIPALS, WE ENCOUNTER BOTH BARRIERS to growing inclusion and allies who support us along the way. Identifying the potential roadblocks and finding the necessary supports are both essential steps for ensuring that inclusion happens in your school.

Overcoming Barriers to Growing Inclusion

The principals I spoke to indicated that they faced a number of common barriers when trying to promote inclusion in their schools. These barriers included: i) Staff members' resistance to change; ii) Staff members' lack of understanding of students' lives; iii) Students' socioeconomic status; iv) Parents who did not feel comfortable with the school; and v) Schools' lack of autonomy to make decisions. Based on my own experiences, I've added two others: v) Bullying, and vi) Principal Burnout.

i) Staff members' resistance to change. Principals cited staff members' resistance to change as a significant barrier to the promotion of inclusion in their schools. This resistance can take the form of disagreement, inertia, or subversion, as the school moves toward more inclusive practices and ways of thinking.

Nigel indicated that there were always staff members who simply did not agree with him on issues of equity in the school. As he explained,

Overcoming Barriers and Cultivating Allies   101

You face [the] barriers of people who don't, fundamentally, agree. Who actually think that, you know, the reason that there's all these black kids in special ed. is either because they're not as smart as white kids, which nobody ever really articulates....or that the conditions within that community are such that they are to blame for the problems that exist.

Some staff members, in other words, felt the system was "just" and that people – black students and people living in the community, in this case – deserved what they got. Nigel always argued his point with these staff members, expressing what he expected in terms of their behaviour, though sometimes that wasn't enough.

You can't control somebody's mind, but you can control, to a certain extent, what they do. I don't think that's an equitable or fair practice. And...whether people just play the game is another issue. It's one of the difficulties we always have [...] whether people really fundamentally change what they believe and think, or whether they just appear to.

So, although Nigel was hopeful that some staff members' resistance would lessen over time, he was not sure whether this was due to compliance, or to their enhanced understanding of the reasons for inclusion. Nonetheless, sometimes compliance with the equity initiative is all that can be achieved, especially in the short term.

Karen discovered that there were staff members who were "normalized into a certain way of doing things." These actions and patterns of thought, she found, were not always conducive to promoting inclusion. A related problem, Karen added, was that since no one had confronted these staff members in the past, they were not accustomed to self-reflection on issues of equity. An important point here is that these patterns of behavior would have been less entrenched had they been confronted earlier.

Allan identified the biggest barrier to inclusion as the "saboteur minority" on staff. As he explained, he was continually confronting

the one or two staff members in the school who just seem to be contentious and oppositional, regardless of what the issue is. If it's black, they say white. If it's up, they say down. Unfortunately, whether it's a character thing, whether it's a personality trait, those saboteurs often tend to be loud, aggressive, and confident people – and they silence the majority. So in that sense alone, getting the majority voice to be heard, or segments of the majority who have important things to say...[can be difficult]

Since these saboteurs' aggressive actions intimidated others and prevented them from speaking up, Allan had to work on getting the majority of staff members to voice their ideas and issues. It was important not only to confront the saboteurs, but also to make certain staff members felt comfortable offering their opinions.

Tony also said that staff members' resistance to change was the biggest barrier he encountered. As he explained,

I think once the staff realizes that the change is beneficial to the kids and to the community, the resistance to change disappears. But resistance to change is a barrier that you have to overcome, and you have to understand why people are resistant to change. You have to – there is the responsibility [to do so]. You have to understand that people have responsibilities within the school, but they also have responsibilities outside the school, in their own personal lives.

Tony acknowledged that part of overcoming this barrier was communicating to staff why change was necessary and how it would benefit students. He told me he always devoted time to explaining the rationale behind a change, as opposed to simply moving forward with it. Tony also remembered that staff members' personal lives could be barriers; some had personal commitments, such as caring for an ailing parent, that limited their ability to participate in school.

Peter described the challenge of working with one experienced teacher who was very resistant to change.

I think with a teacher who is set in their ways, sometimes personality just gets in the way. And you can't change a person's personality. I have a teacher who has been teaching for twenty years, who thinks her way is the right way, and that everything everybody else does is just politics and it just gets in the way of what she wants to do. No matter what I do with that teacher, no matter how I address it, no matter how I approach it, no matter how many olive branches I put out to her, she simply will not move. So what happens is she becomes a negative force on staff and undermines everything that we try to do. But we keep pushing on.

Peter's example served as a reminder that not all staff members will respond to initiatives or strategies for change of any kind. Nonetheless, it is imperative to keep moving forward.

Matt told me that certain staff members at his school were simply resistant to authority. No matter what the issue, he said,

they're going to resist me, and some of them get angry too, yeah. I don't know that they have conscious attitudes of resisting changes for the sake of the children, or [if they're resisting] inclusion and understanding [on principle]. There's, of course, a natural opposition sometimes to something that the principal wants or the leadership wants.

In summary, resistance to change is to be expected, especially when issues or concepts that challenge people's worldviews and past practices are put forth. While it is nice to have everyone on board before moving ahead with inclusion, you should not wait for that. Resistance will decrease once you facilitate learning about inclusion and connect this information to specific actions for staff members. Always make the case for inclusion with direct reference to your school and students.

ii) Staff members' lack of understanding of students' lives. Numerous principals indicated to me that their staff members did not understand their students' lives or experiences, and that this was a main barrier to the promotion of inclusion.

Todd stated that his staff members did not have a clear understanding of what criteria are used to identify a student as being at risk. For that reason, he made it a policy to give staff ideas about how to recognize and connect with at-risk students. As he explained,

> I give them suggestions as to the kinds of things that they could do for a child. For instance, phoning home. Or that they could phone at eight o'clock in the morning to get the kid out of bed so that they can get to school on time. That's not considered to be their job. Their job is to teach them once they get here. So that's sort of something. You know, if they happen to notice that – […] the kid's not bringing a lunch to school, phone home and sort of ask why. Just – I guess maybe what I'm suggesting is, you know, take that extra action, and it's quite often in terms of communication with the home, and just see what they can come up with.

As noted, Todd encouraged staff members to go beyond simply teaching in the classroom. He guided them to connect with the student and the student's family to find solutions and answers. Staff members had to learn about their students' lives outside of school before they could do their best for them in class.

Karen indicated that staff members sometimes thought they were doing the right thing for students when they were, in fact, marginalizing them. She provided the example of a teacher who believed so strongly that her students must be on time for each class that she enforced graduated consequences for each late infraction. The teacher, who came from a middle-class background, firmly believed that she was right to treat the children this way. She did not understand the reality of her students' lives. When one grade eight student was late for the fourth time, for instance, the teacher did not allow him into her class. However, Karen explained,

> the reason that he's late is that his mother leaves for shift work at seven in the morning, [but] they couldn't get a babysitter till nine. So he's responsible for the toddler, his little sister, from seven o'clock till nine o'clock. And, I mean, this is necessary for them to do – so that there can be food on the table, you know. And he's learning good: he's very nurturing with his younger sister, takes very good care of her, walks her to the babysitter, then comes to school. And

> it means he's late. But there's no [sympathy for this from the teacher]. The teacher doesn't know that, because the level of empathy or willingness to consider that there might be reasons for these rules not to be followed [is not there]. So it's a dismissal of a lifestyle.

Even when Karen spoke to the teacher about this student's life, the teacher remained unsympathetic. Despite this, Karen continued to emphasize to the teacher that there were many other factors in students' lives that she needed to consider.

Kristin found that staff members sometimes saw certain children as disruptive and sent them to the office instead of taking extra steps in the classroom to help them. Kristin always advocated for her staff members to support students, especially those students at risk, and to look for solutions. Nonetheless, it was clear to her that staff members did not always understand the students and their needs. For example, she said,

> I have one teacher, who thankfully retires this coming year, I hope, who regularly tells me that she is not a mental health institution and these kids should not be in her classroom, that they should be in other facilities. Whether that is true or not really doesn't matter. The kids are in her classroom and she is the only thing that is really going to be able to help them in this moment in time. Maybe down the road appropriate things will be put in place for that child. But at this time, we need to work through the IEP [individual education plan] process, the IPRC [identification, placement, and review committee] process, and engage with those parents, and keep revising what we are doing and try to make that child successful by affecting the environment that they're in.

This teacher had a specific expectation for the students she wanted to teach; if the students did not fit this mould, she would complain that they should be in places other than her classroom. Kristin, as principal, continued to push this teacher to adapt to students' needs and work with their families to find solutions.

As did many of the other principals, Anna indicated that staff members sometimes lacked the confidence or knowledge to promote real inclusion in the classroom. Special education students, for example, were often placed in the back of the classes, without much support. Anna cited the example of one teacher:

> It's not that she doesn't believe in special ed., but I think she hasn't got a strong background in it and is very curriculum-driven, in terms of her teaching methods, as opposed to being kid-driven and [focused on] what the kids need. And I don't think, I mean, it's not a conscious thing. She is willing to try, but it's baby steps. And I think that's part of it, as well: knowing how far you can push, in terms of what they need to know to do their jobs effectively. And [...] for me, the barrier is time. The time it takes to teach [them].

This teacher did not feel comfortable altering her teaching methods to include more students, especially those with special education concerns. While she was willing to learn new strategies, teaching them to her and to other staff took a lot of time, and put much pressure on Anna.

Susan indicated that her staff members did not always understand the importance of equity issues or the marginalizing effect of cultural norms. She worked with local university professors to increase staff knowledge levels. Bringing in an outside group to teach staff members helped, Susan said, because it created a learning situation for everyone, including her.

Peter indicated that staff members often did not understand much about the lives of the students in the school. He elaborated:

> There are more than one or two on staff [who] don't often realize the situations people face in the community. [...] It's not [the students'] fault [but] [these teachers] often will assign blame, or they'll often [have] negative feelings towards them, and not feel that they need to go out of their way for these kids just because of the socioeconomic difficulties in that community. [They don't realize that] poor people are marginalized in many, many different ways.

Peter added that not every teacher is suited to teaching in all communities; it takes an empathetic teacher, one who is willing to examine how privilege is assigned in our society, to succeed in schools with disadvantaged students. As well, he said, not all staff members understand how to support special education students in their classrooms. On that front, he pointed out,

> They would much rather deal with those average or above average kids, and we'll butt heads, because it is those kids who are special ed. who, when they are marginalized, can often become your behavior problems. They become the ones who go […] looking for attention in negative ways because we're not engaging them properly through the normal routes.

One of the main reasons staff did not engage special education students effectively, Peter said, is that it was simply too much work. Including special education students academically requires developing or modifying programs. Special education students understand very quickly which teachers are frustrated or unwilling to work with them. The result, as Peter pointed out, is behavioural disruptions that are detrimental for everyone in the class.

Matt told me that most of his staff members were white and from middle-class backgrounds, while most of his school's students were neither middle-class nor white. For that reason, staff members did not really understand the lives and experiences of the students.

> There's something of a class distinction that is largely sub-conscious, I think, because people think that they're being generous or open-minded. But they have some reactions towards the way the kids succeed, or [how] the parents behave, not looking at it objectively all the time, and some-times shutting doors because people don't match their expectations.

Matt's staff members based their expectations of students and parents on their lived experiences, not considering that these were less than objective. Matt indicated that he worked with staff to alter these subconscious attitudes toward students and parents.

Understanding our students and their lives is critical, but only once we know ourselves. A building block identified early on in this book is the need to examine our own biases, prejudices, and histories as they connect with the dominant culture in society. Until we do that, we can't truly understand others.

iii) Students' socioeconomic status. Several principals said that the socioeconomic status of students was often a barrier to their inclusion in school.

Kristin made it a point to provide financial support for families in her school who could not afford to pay for student trips; otherwise, she understood, their children would not be included.

Dave, as noted, discovered through interpreters he'd hired that many of the Vietnamese parents in his school were working up to three low-paying jobs just to support their families, which didn't allow them time to participate in the school.

Debra also outlined how parents' work situations limited their participation in school activities. Some special education parents were also unable to attend school council meetings or activities because they did not have transportation. As she explained,

> That distance [between home and school] is just not manageable for some of our families to come in to meet. And that's a whole group that is also excluded because of distance and lack of transportation. So if I know a parent is very interested in coming [or that] we would benefit from hearing this parent's perspective and vice versa, I would just go and drive the parent in, in the evening, for a council meeting.

Debra understood that the parents of bussed students often needed extra help to participate in school activities and she endeavored to create the resources to support them.

Nina identified some of the negative effects of poverty on parental involvement in schools. Parents who were struggling to support their families were less likely to participate, and she explained that these parents often "don't trust anybody. Poverty is very isolating, so when you're living in poverty you've got lots of secrets usually, and you don't want anybody to know them."

The school council at Peter's school comprised of parents from working, educated families, but this was not representative of the school community. Peter tried to get more representation from the other elements of the school population, but was, by his own admission,

> largely unsuccessful, because a lot of those moms are single moms, on social assistance [and] working two jobs, so it is not practical for them to participate. So the barriers of getting those parents involved are significant, and namely because of their socioeconomic status. They don't have the time or the interest to become involved in school because they simply have too many other things on their plate to deal with.

My own experiences as an educator have shown me the often hidden effects of low socioeconomic status: student malnourishment and general lack of food. Many students from poorer areas come to school hungry and remain so for the day. There is a wealth of information outlining the benefits of breakfast, lunch and snack programs in schools, but instituting these programs is problematic given the economic restraints placed on districts. Principals simply do not have the necessary monies in their budgets to allocate the thousands of dollars required to fund these important programs. The answer for most schools in the current climate will involve a combination of local business support, grants, and fund-raising to put together a daily food program that is available to all students. In my schools, the office staff always keeps extra lunches and snacks on hand for students, but one challenge is determining just how many students need this support. If there are fifteen students coming to the office for food each day, for example, it is safe to assume that there are double or triple that number who do not come but should.

iv) Parents not feeling comfortable with the school. This is a very challenging issue. Some parents have been oppressed and marginalized by the school system as children, and these negative experiences are reinforced once they become parents. I do not have a magic solution for breaking down this barrier. The answer is multi-faceted, and it involves making certain that your school does everything it can to make all participants "of" the school, by learning about their life experiences, histories, and cultures, and letting this information inform and shape the way your school operates day to day.

A number of years ago I had a very angry parent come into the main office with her son. She stated quite loudly that the school was racist and that was why her son was not doing well. My first reaction was to be defensive, but thankfully, I chose to respond differently, and I asked them both, mother and son, to join me to talk in my office. In a calm voice, I reiterated the mother's assertion that she felt the school was racist, and asked her to share her thoughts. We talked about forty-five minutes. Mostly, I listened as she described her experiences as a student in the same school district. Her pain was still very evident, and she was worried that her son would have the same experiences. We talked about the current school year and about her son, and I asked her what the school could do better. She was surprised to learn that her views mattered to me, and her insights into school structures and practices that were exclusionary were incisive, as were her ideas about the requisite changes. That was the first of many interactions I had with this parent over my tenure at the school, and her insight and partnership contributed greatly to making the school more inclusive for all students.

Karen talked about the challenge of getting parents to volunteer in her school. She explained,

> Again, that thing about feelings of comfort in the school [comes up]. For some people, school was not an affirming experience, and so they feel out of place there. So [you] always [need to be] sure that you greet people and make it clear that you would value their presence in the school.

On a similar note, Allan pointed out that some parents do not trust schools. As he explained,

A lot of the mistrust in the schools that I've been in is culturally based. Where, you know, parents are coming from
countries [where] [...] institutionalized organizations
like education, policing, military, and so on [play a more
oppressive role in society] [...] And then they come over
here to Canada. They extrapolate that distrust even before
they've met us. And the other side of things is their experiences with other school principals.

Allan worked hard to gain trust in the school community by being consistent and predictable in his dealings with parents.

Debra noted that at her school parents were often concerned that they
would be viewed negatively by staff members, especially if English was not
their first language, or they had not done well in school themselves. They
felt intimidated about interaction with staff members and avoided school
activities because of that. As she explained,

They [parents] are not a regular presence in our school.
Part of it is a language barrier; part of it is an education
[disparity, where the parents think,] "Well, I can't help this
child because I can't even read myself." And part of it is just
fear of parents being evaluated by teachers if they are in
their classroom.

Anna also found that some parents did not feel comfortable at school
because of their own experiences. She highlighted the example of special
education parents.

Many of our special ed. kids' families came from special ed.
backgrounds themselves and, of course, the inclusion piece
was not part of their school experience. And they say, "Well,
I remember getting shoved out and being [excluded]" –
very negative kinds of experiences at school. And [we're]
trying to say that, "No, this is why we're doing it."

Anna tried hard to communicate to these parents that her school was
working to counter negative experiences like these for her students.

Matt also devoted time to communicating with parents about what the school was trying to do for children. As he explained,

> They [the parents] come from something quite different, and they don't understand what we're trying to do, and [they don't understand] our assumptions, [which] have to be explained to them very carefully – especially if it's special ed. or any kind of special help.

v) Schools' lack of autonomy to make decisions. Many of the principals I spoke to felt strongly that schools needed more control over their day-to-day operations and their strategies concerning how best to meet the needs of their students.

Nigel noted that the school system is very much "top-down" and centralized; this took away much control and autonomy from individual schools. He elaborated that there was a "cookie-cutter" approach to school issues, instead of allowing each school to adapt and develop programs to meet its students' needs. Nigel stated,

> I've done a PhD, I mean, for God's sake. I've taught at university for five years. I've read research. I've thought. I've looked at this. Spent a lot of time. I had seventeen years in the classroom. It's ten years since I first became a school administrator. I think I have something to offer. [Yet I feel] totally straitjacketed half the time. I'm trying to do the things that I value on the side. And that's what drives me mad. I don't like doing that and that's why I'm leaving [for another position]. I've done a year [at this school] and I can't stand it. I'm not going to live my life like this. 'Cause I'll end up like a dead body on the side of the road, you know, like road kill. I just have no time to have any life or focus if I'm going to do other things apart from what they want me to do. And inclusion is so not a priority [for them].

Nigel felt that there was little time for him or his school to devote to issues of inclusion because of the emphasis on improving test scores. He suggested that schools would benefit instead from resources, and tools, and supports, and money, and sport, of course. Allow the building of programs [at] the school level and within connections and webs of […] like schools. And giving staff members time and resources to develop that programming, strategies around this and to release some of the control [to the individual schools].

Instead of imposing one approach on all schools, resources would be made available to individual schools to develop programs and curriculums to support their students.

Todd also conveyed concerns about the "one-size-fits-all approach" that schools have to follow. He explained,

It's very difficult to have a template that dictates what every school should have in place. I do believe that every school should have practices in place that reflects [their] community and the students that [they] have.

Karen described the influence of neoliberal ideas in the educational system. Students are seen not for their individual experiences but more as parts of an overall plan. As she stated,

It's a corporate agenda, right? I mean, a lot of what we're doing now is really treating children like lumps of coal to fuel the corporate furnace. To fuel the economy. And that's important to parents, too. Because parents want to see their children have good jobs when they graduate. So it's also a very seductive kind of thing.

Many parents perceive the role of schools as preparing their children for future employment, Karen explained, and this view connects neatly with the neoliberal views. Individual schools do not have enough control over decisions to counter this neoliberal influence, she said.

Many of the important decisions have been taken away from school communities. I mean, our job is to implement what's been decided elsewhere. So when you're promoting inclusion in your school, you're only getting that first half of the definition […]. You're making sure that you include [parents] in the processes that are going on. But the processes themselves don't necessarily promote equity.

Kristin conveyed that, as a principal, she is of "little consequence to the board," which simply follows the system, or the district's orders. She feels the principal is asked to

> "Please just fall in line, and do what you're told, and don't ask questions, and by the way I'd like no parents calling me today." Whether that's the director, the trustees or the superintendent, or whoever [talking, I feel that's the message, even though] I have an entire career invested in education as well, just like they do. And that's how teachers feel, [too].

Even as principal of her school, Kristin did not perceive that she had input into or control over what the district or system was mandating. As she noted, there are many demands placed on principals that have little to do with issues of social justice or inclusion.

There are additional barriers that my research and my own experience generated that merit mentioning here: bullying and principal burnout.

vi) Bullying. A large proportion of elementary school children report being bullied at school, and all the inclusive strategies in the world will not offset the effects of undetected or ignored bullying. Bullying is a common form of exclusion, and it affects not only the victims and the perpetrators, but also the spectators. As Chodzinski (2004) posits,

> Bullying is everyone's problem. Its outcomes are life long and frequently life damaging. Bullying is violent behaviour imposed by individuals who wish to intimidate, harass, alienate and isolate others they perceive as weaker, vulnerable and easy targets (2).

It is imperative to have programs and school-wide foci to support the victims of bullying and identify those who cause harm.

Over the past few years, schools in my district have begun using restorative justice practices both to address issues of violence and also to act as a long-term remedy. I must admit that I was skeptical at first. I was used to giving out suspensions or detentions to address inappropriate behaviour by students. But these past two years have taught me the value and power of using restorative justice practices to address all aspects of school violence. Restorative justice involves both the victims and the perpetrators in exploring the impact of actions and determining how best to make restitution. As Conrad and Unger (2011) assert,

> The use of restorative justice in schools is based on the realization that control, criticism and guilt are not effective ways to change someone's behaviour, but only foster negative self-esteem. Instead the goal of any intervention to an infraction should be self-discipline (55).

Restorative practices are inclusive, and they work to rebuild the community. I have personally witnessed the positive, long-term impact, not only of using restorative language in daily school practice, but also of using restorative circles for seemingly unsolvable chronic disputes and misbehavior.

vii) Principal Burnout

> With rapid changes such as school-centred decision-making, pressure for greater accountability, shrinking resources, and changing demographics, principals are expected to accept more and more responsibilities and the overwhelming task of trying to be all things to all people. How much more can be expected before the daily pressures overshadow the rewards of working with young people? (Whitaker 1992, 115-116)

Although Kathryn Whitaker's important study on principal burnout was published eighteen years ago, her insights are even more applicable today. The demands on principals have increased, and the pressure on principals who promote inclusion is even greater.

For my purposes, I define burnout as "a state of fatigue or frustration brought about by devotion to a cause, way of life, a relationship, that failed to produce expected reward" (Freudenberger 1980, in Whitaker 1995, 287). The relationship between promoting inclusion and principal burnout is unequivocal: nearly seventy-five percent of the principals I spoke to cited serious negative consequences as a result of promoting inclusion. These consequences encompassed everything from discouragement to exhaustion. In all cases, the pursuit of inclusion required the principal to go "above and beyond" what was typically required of a position that is undeniably draining, even without these extra demands.

Because of inclusion's depth and breadth, years are required to build long-term structures that support its presence. The principal needs to be an active part of the process during these years. If the principal "burns out," the promotion of inclusion is likely to stop or be significantly reduced.

As Whitaker (1995) outlined, "Principals are especially susceptible to burnout due to the complex nature of their jobs. Role conflict, role ambiguity, and role overload appear to be particular problems for principals" (Savery & Detiuk, 1986; Murphy, 1994; in Whitaker, 1995, 287). This held true for the principals in my study; many cited examples of role conflict and role overload.

a) **Role conflict**. Role conflict occurs when the roles that the principal must play conflict with one another. Having too many roles means that principals cannot focus or devote sufficient time to *any* of the roles they have. Nigel, for instance, felt frustrated and discouraged that he could not follow through on items he deemed important for his school because the district mandates took up so much time. Issues of equity and inclusion were pushed to the side. As an experienced principal, Nigel believed that his ability to meet his site-specific school needs was being unnecessarily and inefficiently controlled. Similarly, Kristin was frustrated that the "over-prescription" of curriculum prevented her from responding to issues of equity and inclusion in her school. She, too, noted that directives from the district became the foci for the school and conflicted with her ability to promote inclusion. Cushing et al (2003) argue that, for principals,

> stress comes from high levels of responsibility while authority and flexibility are simultaneously reduced via union contracts and fiscal and legal requirements. It [stress] comes from being the first head to roll if reform demands and targets aren't met (29).

Other researchers have also identified the lack of autonomy to meet students' needs and the requirement to implement central-office targets as sources of principals' stress (Johnson 2005; Adamowski and Petrilli 2007). Principals do not have the flexibility to innovate or to attend to issues they deem important because their energies are tied up in meeting the demands of the system. For the principals I spoke to, fostering inclusion was the major issue that fell by the wayside.

Role conflict can also encompass conflicting personal and professional roles (Langer and Boris-Schacter 2003, 17). Debra and Nina both outlined how their family lives had suffered because they spent so much time at school. Even though Nina's family members understood why she spent so much time at school, she said, they had still been affected. Cushing et al. (2003) concur that long hours and the many evenings spent at school are some of the reasons it is not easy to find people who want to become principals (29). Sarros (1988) noted more home-work conflict for principals than for teachers. Women in particular were likely to experience this kind of conflict (in Friedman 1995, 642). Role conflict and the cost to their personal lives can cause principals to question whether they want to remain committed to the organization (Duignan 2006, 28).

b) Role overload. Role overload is a common stressor for school principals, even for those who are not promoting inclusion. In all school districts, there is substantial pressure on principals to implement district and system initiatives while still meeting the many demands of the regular school day. Every day, principals wear many hats: social worker, psychologist, disciplinarian, instructional leader, manager, teacher, etcetera. The demands can be simply overwhelming.

The principals I spoke to, in addition to managing regular duties, also occupied the role of chief promoter of inclusion in their schools. This took time, energy and ongoing commitment. Theoharis' research also finds that the numerous roles played by principals interfere with their promoting social justice (2008, 312).

Promoting inclusion also carries the risk of failure, and some principals I spoke to felt discouraged because their attempts to promote inclusion did not "bear fruit." Anna tried to encourage more parents to participate in the school and was somewhat demoralized when she was not successful. Peter outlined how there were days when it was a challenge to get staff members to support one another or him. Matt tried to encourage staff members to "buy into" inclusion by providing additional support, but even with this added support some still would not participate. All three of these principals highlighted how demanding it was to promote inclusion.

What will happen if these principals come to the point where they simply cannot "go above and beyond" anymore? Given the current mandate of raising student achievement scores, it is not likely in the foreseeable future that principals will have support from the district or system to devote more time to issues of equity, social justice, and inclusion. Yet my research demonstrates the critical importance of principals in the promotion of inclusion in schools. Without their efforts, inclusion will occur, at best, only in pockets of classrooms throughout the school.

Cultivating Allies

The barriers to growing inclusion are very real, as the previous section outlines, but all of the principals I spoke to identified individuals who supported and facilitated the growth of inclusion in their schools. Many of these individuals took leadership roles and worked hard to promote a more inclusive school climate. Principals identified these people as coming from two groups: staff members and parents.

i) **Staff members.** Staff members, particularly teachers, are paramount to growing inclusion at all stages of the process.

Nigel had several strong staff members who volunteered to lead or to be part of different inclusive initiatives at school. These staff members, he explained, organize, and they're people who've picked things up [...] One of the things we've talked about [is] the fact that we want more reverse integration with special education classes. One particular grade three teacher is a first-year teacher who said, "I'm going to [do it]." [So she] spoke to the teacher, the special ed. teacher, and came to me and said, "I'm going to have an ongoing relationship with this MID (mild intellectual disability) class, with my grade three class." Done. And it happened all year, and she just made a decision that she thought it was the right [thing] to do and went ahead and did it.

Karen highlighted the efforts of one teacher who sought to promote inclusion. This teacher led a whole-school initiative to raise money to build a school in another country. Karen outlined how the project came about:

There was one teacher in particular who was the catalyst for it. It was her idea, and so I just did everything I could to throw support behind it. And I invited her and a team of the students that she was working with to school council to present their ideas.

Karen emphasized the importance of the principal providing these "go-to people" on staff with ongoing support so that they could pursue various initiatives.

Other principals also noted the assistance of staff members. Kristin cited the contributions of special education teachers, who were critical to supporting the diverse needs of their students and providing other staff with support. These teachers helped all staff members to support special education students.

Brent had been principal of a variety of schools throughout his career, and he said that at each school there were staff members who supported inclusive views and goals for the school. Having these supportive staff members was vital to moving the school closer to these goals.

Dave noted the importance of the staff members on his school's organizing committee in promoting inclusion. The organizing committee provided guidance and expertise for all staff on building a more inclusive climate. Committee members addressed many aspects of school life, including daily practices. Dave also identified a community-outreach teacher with whom he talked with about "five million times a day" and a M.A.R.T. (Methods and Resource Teacher) as important facilitators of inclusion. He described the work of the M.A.R.T.:

> It was her job to work with the special ed. resource teachers [to] support the integration of the kids. She would organize special ed. staff meetings, where they would talk about all the issues they needed to talk about, paperwork they had to do, and all that stuff. But she also worked with them on how to team-teach, [and helped] all the teachers differentiate their instruction. [Doing] all that kind of stuff was her role.

Allan also outlined the importance of the special education teachers on staff. These teachers provided support to the classroom teachers and often had a better understanding of inclusion than regular classroom teachers did. Their experience ensured that the learning needs of special education students were included in the classroom.

Debra told me that the entire leadership team was critical to growing inclusion in her school. Initially, being on this team of staff members had been a negative experience; a minority of members intimidated other staff members, preventing them from speaking up. Thanks to Debra's efforts, the dynamic changed, and the team as a whole became much more positive, with more staff members voicing their opinions. As she explained,

> We have a lot of people now who are speaking up and saying, "When this happens, this is what this child is feeling – or – when this happens, this is the perception you are giving this child," which is very, very different than it used to be. And they are coming to me now, [to ask] "can we bring such-and-such in and talk about this? Can we purchase these books?"

Tony stated that, initially, there were only two or three key staff members who "were on the same wavelength" in terms of inclusion. These staff members got involved in many different projects. But more staff became involved as time went on, because they believed in the direction the school was going. Tony noticed that if staff members believed the school was "moving in the right direction," they were more likely to take on initiatives. He also underlined the importance of having two or three staff members who were supportive of this direction from the beginning.

Anna identified the special education teacher as her "right hand" person in the school. She consulted daily with this teacher on how to support programming for all students. Susan told me that the staff member who acted as chairperson of her school's equity committee was a powerful facilitator of inclusion. The equity chair coordinated all the initiatives set forth by the equity committee.

Nina said that, in her school, all staff members were supportive of inclusive practices. She cited the example of the free after-school programming for 150 students at the local community centre and added, "Not's everyone's involved in it, but every single one supports it and promotes it." This is an important point; there are different degrees of involvement in growing inclusion. Some staff members will initiate or lead, while others follow; still others will support the activity verbally.

Peter also identified special education teachers as important facilitators in his school. As he explained,

> I think the special ed. teachers do an excellent job communicating and responding to the needs of those kids who are excluded by promoting it [solutions] with the staff.

The special education teachers at Peter's school worked with staff members to support the differentiation of programs and other ways of servicing students who were at risk academically.

Matt stated that he was fortunate in that "key" positions in his schools were always filled by staff members who advocated for inclusion. These staff members, he explained,

> are in those positions, like the special ed. coordinator, literacy coordinator, and kindergarten teachers. [They] are the

parents' first contact with the school and remain the most important person in their memory even six years later, because everybody has gone through the kindergarten, and then the siblings come through, and so that's kind of your entry point. Psychologically, it's your entry point into the school for the families.

This positive first experience with school is especially important if the parents' own educational experiences were not positive ones, Matt pointed out.

Craig identified his allies as the individuals who chaired the different areas of the school. As he elaborated,

I try to put people in successful positions, or set them up for success, wholly and knowing full well that I want them to be even better than me. We have what's called in our school "champions." Our champions literally run the school. So these are people that I call champions – like in front of staff and everyone. They know Michelle [for instance] is one of the major champions of our school as far as our setting up of professional learning communities [goes].

The champions of each area met regularly for a "core of champions" meeting, Craig told me. He developed his allies of inclusion through this "champions" framework, and these staff members were provided with decision-making power and budget support.

ii) Parents. The principals I spoke to also mentioned that parents could be strong facilitators of inclusion in their schools. Some of these parents joined school councils or parent-teacher associations and used these positions to facilitate inclusion.

Todd stated that, in the previous two years, his school council chairs had been outstanding. As he explained, these chairs had distinguished themselves by being

big on fundraising [and] big on graduation planning. They're big on political turnarounds, or events that are occurring, or policy, and health and safety is another one

[of their areas of emphasis]. They have their own committees [in] each of those areas, too.

The school council chairs provided opportunities through these various committees for other parents to participate. They were also active in the opposite direction: they became involved in board policy and its subsequent impact on the school.

Tony identified one of his student's grandmothers, a retired principal from Trinidad, as a terrific facilitator of inclusion. As he stated,

> I had a lot of discussions with her, lots of discussions. And she was really instrumental in helping me to sort of move things ahead, because she was the quiet voice that would come in and say, well, how about this? We tried to start a steel band, steel drummers. It was too expensive, couldn't do it. But she would come in with the greatest ideas, and we would move with them.

Tony was able to use this grandparent's knowledge and experience to help connect with the community and the students. He also had some very talented school council chairs who were supportive of the school. One of these council chairs met with parents and community members on Saturdays to glean their ideas and opinions.

Anna also noted that her school council members had been strong facilitators for inclusion in the school. The previous year, however, had been different, since Anna found she could not depend on her school council members as much due to their work responsibilities outside of school. As she explained,

> This year, they are all working full time, and it's been kind of difficult to get that communication out there. It was better last year when, I would say, three out of seven were working and the rest weren't. Now they're all working. And of course, when you're working fulltime and trying to take that on, it's been a bit of a struggle.

Susan identified several parents as excellent liaisons with the school community. These parents connected with parents in languages other than English, then shared the information with the principal. The liaison allowed many parents who did not have strong English language skills to have their voices heard.

Nina described the dedication of some of her parents to the daily snack program at her school. The snack program required a considerable financial commitment, costing $20,000 per year to operate. A couple of parents drove their cars each day to pick up and deliver food to the school. This was a year-long, nearly daily commitment for them.

Matt noted that his school council chair was an excellent facilitator of inclusion. The council chair had a lot of influence with the parents, especially those within his own ethnic group. He was able to communicate what was happening in the school and supported parents' participation in school events and activities.

In all cases, the key aspect to identifying allies was the principal knowing both his or her staff members and the parents in the school. Knowing involves finding out who staff members and parents are as people, and drawing on their talents, experiences, and interests. In every school there are staff members and parents who are social justice advocates; the challenge, if they do not self-identify, is to find them. In my schools, I have spotted potential advocates through my daily discourse with them and through hearing their input during whole-staff discussions at meetings or professional development activities. It is important to start small, with a couple of staff members working with you at the start, to grow inclusion. More will join once you demonstrate the urgency of the need for your school and identify specific actions. Keep in mind that some staff will never join in, regardless of the learning opportunities you facilitate. Stay positive and work with those who are committed to the process.

Reconceptualising the Principalship

> There are a vast number of people who are uninformed
> and heavily propagandized, but fundamentally decent. The
> propaganda that inundates them is effective when unchal-
> lenged, but much of it goes only skin deep. If they can be
> brought to raise questions and apply their decent instincts
> and basic intelligence, many people quickly escape the con-
> fines of the doctrinal system and are willing to do some-
> thing to help others who are really suffering and oppressed.
> (Chomsky, as cited in Achbar 1994, 195)

THERE IS HOPE FOR THE FUTURE OF INCLUSION and it is anchored
in our understanding of the world around us. This understanding involves
learning how societal forces construct the world so as to limit and constrain individuals and groups. Given the propensity and power of deficit
ideologies, and beliefs that North America is a meritocracy, knowledge
of these societal forces is really not widely held. Once such knowledge is
grasped and understood, I fully expect educators to become advocates of
inclusion and social justice. But these new understandings take time to
grow and even more time before they will bear fruit.

As principals, we need to concentrate on the "why" of education. Growing
inclusion demands that we change how we conceptualize our roles as principals and our purposes within the system. In this regard, we have important roles to play as public intellectuals, critiquing an education system
that focuses on efficiency and quantitative data rather than on serving our

students in a holistic way. Assuming this role is critical to our becoming empowering advocates for inclusion in our schools.

While there are many conceptions of the public intellectual, I like Said's (1994) definition:

> The intellectual is an individual endowed with a faculty for representing, embodying, articulating a message, a view, an attitude, philosophy or opinion to, as well as for, a public. And this role has an edge to it, and cannot be played without a sense of being someone whose place it is publically to raise embarrassing questions, to confront orthodoxy and dogma (rather than to produce them), to be someone who cannot easily be co-opted by governments or corporations, and whose raison d'etre is to represent all those people and issues that are routinely forgotten or swept under the rug. The intellectual does so on the basis of universal principles: that all human beings are entitled to expect decent standards of behaviour concerning freedom and justice from worldly powers or nations, and that deliberate or inadvertent violations of these standards need to be testified and fought against courageously (10).

As principals and public intellectuals, we must advocate for all of our students, especially those who are marginalized and excluded by the current educational system. Moreover, we must resist the pressures of our districts and accompanying system directives that conflict with these universal principles of freedom and justice. In certain cases, we will have to confront our employers to uphold these principles. This will be challenging for many of us. Typically, the principalship is characterized by the imperative to maintain order and control in schools, which in turn supports and secures the status quo.

In order for us to fulfill our role as public intellectuals, ongoing learning is required. We need to develop a comprehensive understanding of how societal issues and institutions affect schools, more specifically the learning experiences and possibilities of all students. Our training and study is never complete, because the issues that affect our students are always in a state of flux. As Barth states,

> What is desperately needed in deliberation about our
> reform in our nation's schools is a continual conversation
> between social science research and craft knowledge, and
> between social scientist and educator. Each has tough and
> important questions to ask the other (in Mai 2004, 4).

These discussions must stay current if they are to prepare principals and our staff members adequately for each school day. Giroux (1997) asserts that, as educators, we constantly examine the relations between culture and power in society. Our failure to understand how these relations shape, constrain, and reproduce existing inequities will doom any attempt at educational reform (130).

As principals, we must take the lead – at least initially – in promoting inclusion, and work to make it a reality in our schools. We are building this framework for the long term. Without a working model of inclusion, a school can generate excellent numbers on tests but continue the patterns of exclusion. I want all of my students to be literate writers and readers, but I also want them to think for themselves, to believe in themselves, and to refuse to be defined or marginalized by deficit ideologies and practices.

Consistent with Said's definition, teachers, students, parents and community members can also become public intellectuals. This, too, is essential to the long-term sustainability of inclusion.

As principals, we are made to work within a system of market accountability. Yet we must ensure that inclusion is at the forefront. To do this, we must subvert the system. I see the process as akin to stickhandling in hockey, where the object is to protect the puck from your opponents within the rules of the game. As principals, we must shield our commitment to inclusion so that it is not overpowered by the many systemic demands and constraints we face. As Rapp (2002) writes,

> If there are fewer and fewer cracks from which to develop
> consciousness, resistance, subversion, and libratory action
> against systemic injustice in schools, universities, and
> professional associations, educators committed to critical
> pedagogies and social justice must respond by gravitating

to groups and sites where they can form coalitions, confidence, and positions of power (228).

As principals, we need to develop coalitions within our schools to build support for social justice. Using the strategies I've outlined in this book, we can work to include all students, staff, parents, and community members in our schools.

Are schools responsible for more than improving results on test scores? Of course they are. Do the achievement gaps among student groups stem from systemic and discriminatory processes in both our educational systems and the larger society? Yes, undoubtedly they do. Once we understand that, we can begin to change it. As principals, we can work to create an education system that truly serves our students, a system that is equitable, inclusive and socially just.

Afterword

BEING A SCHOOL PRINCIPAL can be rewarding work. Frequently, people who take on this role talk about how wonderful they feel about working with a terrific group of teachers who have the best interests of students and parents at the heart of their daily work. Sometimes, school principals talk about the excitement of working in a school division or system where the administrators are fostering positive educational directions. Seldom, in public ways, do we encounter a discussion of the role confusion or conflict, overload, isolation, and contestations that many school principals experience.

The chapters in this book provide a refreshing, and in my view entirely accurate and revealing, conversation about many of the positive and the negative experiences of a group of urban school principals who discuss what it has meant for them to strive to foster a philosophy of inclusion in their schools.

As the sub-title suggests, this book is full of practical suggestions. It also dips into a number of grey areas about doing the work of a school principal. Talk about these grey areas is frequently muted or left out in much of the literature on school leadership. While the principals whose voices are heard in this book talk about the need to place "absent voices" of some marginalized students and parents into school discourses, it strikes me that the voices of these principals break through a barrier and lay out for scrutiny a number of important topics for all of us who wish to improve schools.

There are, of course, easy ways to be a school principal. You can emphasize test scores and focus on quantitative data about students and their progress. You can insist on curriculum specializations and rigor. You can be a "follower" and serve the dominant voices within your staff or within the larger system. You can believe that "merit" will ultimately sort and sift the students, parents and staff in your school into those who deserve your time and effort and those who do not.

However, none of the people who speak out in this book see these as the routes to being a "good principal." Instead, they talk about holistic views of education, inclusive leadership, social justice, restorative justice, anti-bullying, diversity as norm, and their work in schools as a complicated uneven process that requires deep listening, open doors, strategic hiring, countering resistance and acknowledging marginalization as an integral, if difficult to see, part of the overarching "system" in which the schools are immersed.

The overall vision espoused by Dr. Griffiths and the people he interviewed is attractive. It posits that ALL students and parents must be valued and accommodated. It challenges the school principal to stand up and be counted as a "public intellectual" and beyond that to afford the parents, teachers and students in the school the room and encouragement to do the same. The view shared across the people who speak out in this book is that ALL students ought to be active participants in the life of the school.

The practical strategies laid out in the book offer not only hope and encouragement to those who wish to take up the challenge put forth by this vision, they offer important elements that can lead to success in striving to reach such lofty goals. There is much talk about allies, coalitions and fostering positive positions of power and confidence for teachers, students and parents. There is also strategic advice about how to handle those who, for a variety of reasons, are likely to try to subvert this vision and all efforts to actualize it.

As someone who has spent a long and fulfilling career in a variety of educational roles striving to foster inclusion, this book offers hope for a continuation of such efforts. The book also offers some refreshing new voices and perspectives that are rooted in daily school realities, during an era when we are all experiencing flux and challenge. I wish to thank Dr. Griffiths for compiling the book, and thank all those who contributed their voices to the project. With people like these in our school leadership roles, ALL students have the chance of being the strong contributors to our future society that the 21st century demands of them and of those of us who work with them in schools.

Dr. Cecilia Reynolds, Dean, College of Education,
University of Saskatchewan

References

Achbar, Mark. (Ed.). 1994. *Manufacturing consent: Noam Chomsky and the media.* Montreal, Quebec, Canada: Black Rose Books.

Adamowski, Steven, and Michael J. Petrilli. 2007. "Confronting the autonomy gap." *Principal,* 87(2): 46-49.

Alway, Joan. 1995. *Critical theory and political possibilities: conceptions of emancipatory politics in the works of Horkeimer, Adorno, Marcuse, and Harbermas.* Westport, CT: Greenwood Press.

Anyon, Jean. 2005. *Radical Possibilities.* New York: Routledge.

Anyon, Jean. 1997. *Ghetto Schooling: A political economy of urban educational reform.* New York: Teachers College Press.

Capper, Colleen. A., George Theoharis, and James Sebastian. 2006. "Toward a ramework for preparing leaders for social justice." *Journal of Educational Administration,* 44(3): 209-224.

Chodzinksi, Raymond.T. 2004. *Bullying: a crisis in our schools and our communities.* Welland, Ontario: Soleil.

Conrad, Diane, and Dianne Unger. 2011. "Violence at school, the violence of schooling: restorative alternatives." In *International Perspectives in Restorative Justice in Education,* edited by John Charlton, Sandra Pavelka, and Phillip Verrecchia, 30-69. Kanata, Ontario: J Charlton Publishing Ltd.

Cohen, Rosetta. 2002. "Schools our teachers deserve: a proposal for teacher-centred reform." *Phi Delta Kappan,* 83(7):532-537.

Cooper, Jewell E., Ye He., and Barbara B. Levin. 2011. *Developing critical cultural competence: a guide for 21st-century educators.* Thousand Oaks, CA: Corwin Press.

Covey, Stephen. R. 1990. *Seven habits of highly effective people: Power lessons in personal change.* St. Louis, Mo.: San Val, Inc.

Cushing, Katherine. S., Judith A. Kerrins, and Thomas Johnstone. 2003. "Disappearing Principals." *Leadership,* 32(5): 28-29, 37.

Daniel, Beverly-Jean. 2007. "Developing educational collectives and networks: Moving beyond the boundaries of "community" in urban education." In *Urban Teacher Education and Teaching: Innovative Practices for Diversity and Social Justice,* edited by R. Patrick Solomon and Dia N. R. Sekayi, 31-47. New Jersey: Lawrence Erlbaum Associates.

Deal, Terrence .E., and Kent D. Peterson. 2009. *Shaping school culture: Pitfalls, paradoxes, & Promises.* San Francisco, CA: Jossey Bass.

Diangelo, Robin. J. 2006. " 'I'm leaving': White fragility in racial dialogues." In, *Inclusion in urban educational environments: Addressing issues of diversity, equity, and social justice*, edited by Denise E. Armstrong and Brenda J. McMahon, 213-240 . Charlotte, NC: Information Age Publishing.

Duignan, Patrick. 2006. *Educational leadership: Key challenges and ethical tensions.* Port Melbourne: Cambridge University Press.

Durden, Tonia. 2008. "Do your homework! Investigating the role of culturally relevant pedagogy in comprehensive school reform models serving diverse student populations." *Urban Review*, 40: 403-419.

Evans, Andrea. E. 2007. "School leaders and their sensemaking about race and demographic change." *Educational Administration Quarterly,* 43(2): 159-188.

Ferlazzo, Larry, and Lorrie Hammond. 2009. *Building Parent Engagement in Schools.* Santa Barbara, CA: Linworth Publishing.

Ferguson, Diane. L. 1996. "Is it inclusion yet? Bursting the bubbles." In *Stories of Inclusion, change and renewal,* edited by Michael Berres, Dianne L. Ferguson, Peter Knoblock, and Connie Woods, 16- 38. New York: Teachers College Press.

Fossey, Richard. 2003. "School desegregation is over in the inner cities: What do we do now?" In *Reinterpreting Urban School Reform,* edited by Louis F. Miron, and Edward P. St. John, 15-32. Albany: State University of New York Press

Friedman, Issac. A. 1995. "Measuring school principal-experienced burnout." *Educational and Psychological Measurement,* 55(4): 641-655.

Fullan, Michael. 2011. *Change Leader: Learning to do what matters most.* San Francisco, CA: Jossey-Bass.

Giroux, Henry. 1997. *Pedagogy and the politics of hope.* Boulder, Colorado: Westview Press.

Goodman, Diane. J. 2001. *Promoting diversity and social justice: Educating people from privileged groups.* Thousand Oaks, CA: Sage Publications, Inc.

Grant, Kathy B., and Julie A. Ray. 2010. *Home, School, and Community Collaboration: Culturally Responsive Family Involvement.* Thousand Oaks, CA: Sage Publications, Inc.

Howard, Tyrone C. 2003. "Culturally relevant pedagogy: Ingredients for critical teacher reflection." *Theory into Practice,* 42(3): 195-202.

Johnson, Lori A. 2005. "Why principals quit." *Principal,* 84(3): 21-23.

Kazemipur, Abdolmohammad, and Shiva S. Halli. 2000. *The New Poverty in Canada: Ethnic groups and Ghetto Neighbourhoods.* Toronto: Thompson Educational Publishing, Inc.

Langer, Sondra, and Sheryl Boris-Schacter. 2003. "Challenging the image of the American principalship." *Principal*, 83(1): 14-18.

Lee, Kevin. 2000. *Urban Poverty in Canada: A Statistical Profile*. Canadian Council on Social Development.

Loder, Tondra. L. 2006. "Dilemmas confronting urban principals in the post-civil rights era." In *The Praeger Handbook of Urban Education, Volume 1*, edited by Joe L. Kincheloe, Kecia Hayes, Karel Rose, and Philip M. Anderson, 71-77. Westport, Connecticut: Greenwood Press.

Mai, Robert. (2004). "Leadership for school improvement: Cues from organizational learning and renewal efforts." *The Educational Forum*, 68(3):211-221.

Martusewicz, Rebecca A., and William M. Reynolds. 1994. "Turning the study of education inside/out." In *Contemporary critical perspectives in Education*, edited by Rebecca A. Martusewicz and William M. Reynolds, 1-20. New York: St. Martin's Press.

Matthews, Joe, and Gary M. Matthews. 2010. *The Principalship: New Roles in a Professional Learning Community*. New York: Allyn & Bacon.

Maynes, Mary Jo, Jennifer L. Pierce, and Barbara Laslett. 2008. *Telling stories: the use of personal narratives in the social sciences and history*. Ithaca, NY: Cornell University Press.

McGahan, Peter. 1995. *Urban Sociology in Canada* (3rd Ed.). Toronto: Harcourt Brace & Company.

McIntosh, Peggy. 1998. "White privilege: Unpacking the invisible knapsack." *Peace and Freedom* (July/August): 10-12.

Miller, John P. 1993. *The Holistic Teacher*. OISE Press: Toronto: OISE Press.

Milner, H. Richard. 2011. "Culturally relevant pedagogy in a diverse urban classroom." *Urban Review*, 43: 66-89.

Olender, Rosemary A., Jacquelyn Elias, and Rosemary Mastroleo. 2010. *The School- Home Connection: Forging Positive Relationships with Parents*. Thousand Oaks, CA: Corwin.

Popkewitz, Thomas S. 1999. Critical traditions, modernisms, and the "posts". In *Critical theories in education, changing terrains of knowledge and politics*, edited by Thomas S. Popekwitz and Lynn Fendler, 1-13. New York: Routledge.

Portelli, John. P., R. Patrick Solomon. 2001. "Introduction." In *The Erosion of Democracy of Education: From Critique to Possibilities*, edited by John P. Portelli and R. Patrick Solomon, 15-27. Calgary: Detselig Enterprises Ltd.

Quinn, Terrence. 2002. "Redefining leadership in the standards era." *Principal*, 82(1): 16-20.

Rapp, Dana. 2002. "Social justice and the importance of rebellious, oppositional imaginations." *Journal of school leadership,* 12(3): 226-245.

Robinson, Viviane. 1994. "The practical promise of critical research in educational administration." *Educational Administration Quarterly,* 30(1): 56-76.

Russo, Charles. J., and Bruce S. Cooper. 1999. "Prologue: Understanding urban education today." *Urban and Education Society,* 31(2): 131-144.

Ryan, James. 2006a. "Inclusive leadership and social justice for schools." *Leadership and Policy in Schools,* 5(1): 3-15.

-------- 2006b. "Exclusion in urban schools and communities. In *Inclusion in urban educational environments: Addressing issues of diversity, equity, and social justice,* edited by Denise E. Armstrong and Brenda J. McMahon, 3-30 .Charlotte, NC: Information Age Publishing.

-------- 2006c. *Inclusive Leadership.* Toronto: Jossey-Bass.

-------- 2003. *Leading diverse schools.* Boston: Kluwer Academic Publishers.

Said, Edward W. 1994. *Representations of the Intellectual: The 1993 Reith Lectures.* London: Vintage.

Salend, Spencer. 2005. *Creating Inclusive Classrooms,* (5th Ed). Toronto: Pearson Education Inc.

Theobald, Paul. (2005). Urban and rural schools: Overcoming lingering obstacles. *Phi Delta Kappan,* 87(2): 116-122.

Theoharis, George. 2008. " 'At every turn': The resistance that principals face in their pursuit of equity and justice." *Journal of School Leadership,* 18(3):303-343

Thoreau, Henry. D. 1993. *Faith in a seed: The dispersion of seeds and other late natural history writings.* Island Press.

Veck, Wayne. 2009. "Listening to include." *International Journal of Inclusive Education,* 13(2): 141-155.

Vojtek, RoseAnne O'Brien., and Robert J. Vojtek. 2009. *Motivate! Inspire! Lead! 10 Strategies to building collegial learning communities.* Thousand Oaks, CA: Corwin.

Ware, Linda. 1995. "The aftermath of the articulate debate: the invention of inclusive education." In *Towards inclusive schools?* Edited by Catherine Clark, Alan Dyson, and Allan Millware, 127-146. New York: Teachers College Press.

Whitaker, Kathryn. S. 1995. "Principal burnout: Implications for professional development." *Journal of Personnel Evaluation in Education,* 9(3): 287-296.

-------- 1992. "The elusive phenomenon of principal burnout." *NASSP Bulletin,* 76 (547): 112-116.

Wotherspoon, Terry. 2004. *The sociology of education in Canada: Critical perspectives* (2nd Ed.). Toronto: Oxford University Press.

Zepeda, Sally J. 2004. "Leadership to build learning communities." *The Educational Forum*, 68(2): 144-151.

About the Author

Darrin Griffiths has worked as an educator in urban elementary schools for more than twenty years, as a teacher, a vice-principal and a principal. He is a critical pragmatist with a solid understanding of the complex nature of schooling and a commitment to equity for all students. Griffiths obtained his Ed.D from the Ontario Institute for Studies in Education. He lives with his family in Burlington, Ontario, and he is currently the principal of Queen Mary School in nearby Hamilton.

CPSIA information can be obtained at www.ICGtesting.com
Printed in the USA
LVOW120122020513

331866LV00006B/36/P